# Language Skills Practice
# Grammar, Usage, and Mechanics

Perfection Learning®

© 2011 Perfection Learning® Corporation
The purchase of this book entitles an individual teacher to reproduce pages for use in the classroom. This permitted use of copyrighted material does not extend beyond the building level. Reproduction for use in an entire school system or for commercial use is prohibited. Beyond the classroom use by an individual teacher, reproduction, transmittal, or retrieval of this work is prohibited without written permission from the publisher.

Printed in the United States of America.

1 2 3 4 5 6 WC 16 15 14 13 12 11

For information, contact
**Perfection Learning® Corporation**
1000 North Second Avenue, P.O. Box 500
Logan, Iowa 51546-0500
Phone: 1-800-831-4190 • Fax: 1-800-543-2745
perfectionlearning.com

77906
ISBN-13: 978-0-7891-7909-8
ISBN-10: 0-7891-7909-1

# Table of Contents

## Grammar

### Chapter 14 The Sentence
Recognizing Sentences .................... 5
Subjects and Predicates .................... 6
Complete Subjects........................ 7
Simple Subjects........................... 8
Complete Predicates...................... 9
Simple Predicates, or Verbs............... 10
Complete and Simple Subjects
  and Predicates ....................... 11
Verb Phrases ............................ 12
Interrupted Verb Phrases ................ 13
Different Positions of Subjects ........... 14
Compound Subjects ..................... 15
Compound Verbs......................... 16
Kinds of Sentences ...................... 17
The Sentence Review .................... 18

### Chapter 15 Nouns and Pronouns
Nouns ................................... 19
Compound Nouns ....................... 20
Common and Proper Nouns............... 21
Pronoun Antecedents.................... 22
Personal Pronouns....................... 23
Reflexive and Intensive Pronouns......... 24
Other Kinds of Pronouns................. 25
Nouns and Pronouns Review ............ 26

### Chapter 16 Verbs
Action Verbs ......................... 27–28
Transitive and Intransitive Verbs.......... 29
Helping Verbs .......................... 30
Linking Verbs ....................... 31–32
Linking Verb or Action Verb?.......... 33–34
Verbs Review............................ 35

### Chapter 17 Adjectives and Adverbs
Adjectives................................ 36
Different Positions of Adjectives........... 37
Proper Adjectives........................ 38
Adjective, Noun, or Pronoun?.......... 39–40
Adverbs.............................. 41–42
Adverbs That Modify Verbs ............... 43
Adverbs That Modify Adjectives and
  Other Adverbs ....................... 44
Adjectives and Adverbs Review........... 45

### Chapter 18 Other Parts of Speech
Prepositions.......................... 46–47
Prepositional Phrases .................... 48

Preposition or Adverb?................... 49
Conjunctions and Interjections ........... 50
Prepositions, Conjunctions, and
  Interjections Review................... 51
Other Parts of Speech Review ........... 52

### Chapter 19 Complements
Direct Objects ........................... 53
Indirect Objects ......................... 54
Direct and Indirect Objects............... 55
Predicate Nominatives ................... 56
Predicate Adjectives ..................... 57
Complements Review.................... 58

### Chapter 20 Phrases
Prepositional Phrases .................... 59
Adjectival Phrases ................... 60–61
Misplaced Adjectival Phrases ............. 62
Adverbial Phrases .................... 63–64
Appositives and Appositive Phrases........ 65
Phrases Review.......................... 66

### Chapter 21 Verbals and Verbal Phrases
Participles................................ 67
Participle or Verb? ....................... 68
Participial Phrases ....................... 69
Misplaced Participial Phrases.............. 70
Infinitives ............................... 71
Infinitive or Prepositional Phrase?......... 72
Infinitive Phrases ........................ 73
Verbals and Verbal Phrases Review ....... 74

### Chapter 22 Clauses
Independent and Subordinate Clauses...... 75
Adverbial Clauses........................ 76
Subordinating Conjunctions............... 77
Adjectival Clauses ....................... 78
Misplaced Adjectival Clauses ............. 79
Simple and Compound Sentences ......... 80
Compound Sentence or Compound Verb?... 81
Complex Sentences ...................... 82
Clauses Review .......................... 83

### Chapter 23 Sentence Fragments
### and Run-ons
Sentence Fragments .................. 84–85
Phrase Fragments ....................... 86
Clause Fragments........................ 87
Run-on Sentences ....................... 88
Sentence Fragments and Run-ons Review... 89

*continued*

# Table of Contents *continued*

## Usage

### Chapter 24 Using Verbs
The Principal Parts of Verbs . . . . . . . . . . . . 90–91
Regular Verbs . . . . . . . . . . . . . . . . . . . . . . . . 92–93
Irregular Verbs . . . . . . . . . . . . . . . . . . . . . . . 94–95
Six Problem Verbs . . . . . . . . . . . . . . . . . . . . . . . 96
Verb Tense . . . . . . . . . . . . . . . . . . . . . . . . . . . 97–98
Shifts in Tense . . . . . . . . . . . . . . . . . . . . . . . . . . 99
Progressive Verb Forms . . . . . . . . . . . . . . . . . . 100
Using Verbs Review . . . . . . . . . . . . . . . . . . . . . 101

### Chapter 25 Using Pronouns
Identifying the Cases of
 Personal Pronouns . . . . . . . . . . . . . . 102–103
Pronouns Used as Subjects . . . . . . . . . . . . . . . 104
Pronouns Used as Predicate Nominatives . . 105
Pronouns Used as Direct and
 Indirect Objects . . . . . . . . . . . . . . . . . . . . . 106
Pronouns Used as Objects
 of Prepositions . . . . . . . . . . . . . . . . . . . . . . 107
The Possessive Case . . . . . . . . . . . . . . . . . . . . . 108
Possessive Pronoun or Contraction? . . . . . . . 109
Pronouns and Their Antecedents . . . . . . . . . . 110
Indefinite Pronouns as Antecedents . . . . . . . 111
Unclear or Missing Antecedents . . . . . . . . . . 112
Using Pronouns Review . . . . . . . . . . . . . . . . . 113

### Chapter 26 Subject and Verb Agreement
Number . . . . . . . . . . . . . . . . . . . . . . . . . . . 114–115
Singular and Plural Subjects . . . . . . . . . 116–117
Verb Phrases . . . . . . . . . . . . . . . . . . . . . . . . . . . 118
Agreement with Contractions . . . . . . . . . . . . 119
Interrupting Words . . . . . . . . . . . . . . . . . . . . . 120
Inverted Order . . . . . . . . . . . . . . . . . . . . . . . . . 121
Compound Subjects . . . . . . . . . . . . . . . . 122–123
Collective Nouns . . . . . . . . . . . . . . . . . . . . . . . 124
*You* and *I* as Subjects . . . . . . . . . . . . . . . . . . . 125
Indefinite Pronouns . . . . . . . . . . . . . . . . . . . . 126
Subject and Verb Agreement Review . . . . . . 127

### Chapter 27 Using Adjectives and Adverbs
Comparison of Adjectives and Adverbs . . . . 128
Degree of Comparison . . . . . . . . . . . . . . 129–130
Irregular Comparison . . . . . . . . . . . . . . . . . . . 131
*Other* and *Else* . . . . . . . . . . . . . . . . . . . . . . . . . 132
Double Comparisons and
 Double Negatives . . . . . . . . . . . . . . . 133–134
*Good* or *Well?* . . . . . . . . . . . . . . . . . . . . . . . . . . 135
Using Adjectives and Adverbs Review . . . . . 136

## Mechanics

### Chapter 28 Capital Letters
First Words and the Pronoun *I* . . . . . . . . . . . . 137
Proper Nouns . . . . . . . . . . . . . . . . . . . . . 138–139
Proper Adjectives . . . . . . . . . . . . . . . . . . 140–141
Titles . . . . . . . . . . . . . . . . . . . . . . . . . . . . . . . . . 142
Titles of Works . . . . . . . . . . . . . . . . . . . . . . . . . 143
Capital Letters Review . . . . . . . . . . . . . . . . . . 144

### Chapter 29 End Marks and Commas
End Marks . . . . . . . . . . . . . . . . . . . . . . . . 145–146
Periods with Abbreviations . . . . . . . . . . . . . . 147
Commas with a Series . . . . . . . . . . . . . . . 148–149
Adjectives Before a Noun . . . . . . . . . . . . . . . . 150
Compound Sentences . . . . . . . . . . . . . . . 151–152
Introductory Elements . . . . . . . . . . . . . . 153–154
Dates, Addresses, and Letters . . . . . . . . . . . . 155
Parenthetical Expressions . . . . . . . . . . . 156–157
Appositives and Nonessential
 Elements . . . . . . . . . . . . . . . . . . . . . . 158–159
End Marks and Commas Review . . . . . . 160–161

### Chapter 30 Italics and Quotation Marks
Italics (Underlining) and Quotation Marks
 with Titles . . . . . . . . . . . . . . . . . . . . . . 162–163
Direct and Indirect Quotations . . . . . . . . . . . 164
Capital Letters with Direct Quotations . . . . . 165
Commas and End Marks with Direct
 Quotations . . . . . . . . . . . . . . . . . . . . . . . . . 166
Writing Dialogue . . . . . . . . . . . . . . . . . . . . . . . 167
Italics and Quotation Marks
 Review . . . . . . . . . . . . . . . . . . . . . . . . 168–169

### Chapter 31 Other Punctuation
Apostrophes . . . . . . . . . . . . . . . . . . . . . . 170–171
Possessive Forms of Pronouns . . . . . . . . . . . . 172
Contraction or Possessive Pronoun? . . . . . . . 173
Apostrophes with Certain Plurals . . . . . . . . . 174
Semicolons and Colons . . . . . . . . . . . . . 175–176
Hyphens . . . . . . . . . . . . . . . . . . . . . . . . . . . . . . 177
Other Punctuation Review . . . . . . . . . . . 178–179

### Chapter 32 Spelling
Spelling Patterns . . . . . . . . . . . . . . . . . . . 180–181
Plurals . . . . . . . . . . . . . . . . . . . . . . . . . . . 182–184
Prefixes and Suffixes . . . . . . . . . . . . . . . . 185–187
Spelling Review . . . . . . . . . . . . . . . . . . . . . . . . 188

### Appendix
Power Rules . . . . . . . . . . . . . . . . . . . . . . 189–193
Power Rules Review . . . . . . . . . . . . . . . . . . . . 194

Name _____  Date _____

## CHAPTER 14 — Recognizing Sentences

**[14A]** A **sentence** is a group of words that expresses a complete thought.

**[14A.1]** A group of words that expresses an incomplete thought is called a **sentence fragment**.

> **EXERCISE** Label each group of words S if it is a sentence or F if it is a sentence fragment.

_____ 1. Lion cubs play like kittens.

_____ 2. Met up with Nate's friends at the park.

_____ 3. The girl wearing the blue sweater.

_____ 4. Look both ways before crossing the street.

_____ 5. There were long lines at the store.

_____ 6. Under the papers on the dining room table.

_____ 7. Seahorses cling to underwater plants.

_____ 8. Exciting action-adventure books and movies.

_____ 9. The players on the basketball team.

_____ 10. We are leaving at seven o'clock.

_____ 11. Show me how to sew a scarf and mittens.

_____ 12. Made a lot of progress during practice.

Name _____ Date _____

# CHAPTER 14  Subjects and Predicates

**[14B]** The **subject** of a sentence names the person, place, thing, or idea that the sentence is about.
**[14C]** The **predicate** tells what the subject is or does.

> **EXERCISE** Identify each underlined word as the subject, predicate, or neither.

_____ 1. Squirrels <u>nibble</u> nuts and seeds.
  A  subject
  B  predicate
  C  neither

_____ 2. The <u>Sahara</u> has very little rain.
  A  subject
  B  predicate
  C  neither

_____ 3. Most robins <u>fly</u> south for the winter.
  A  subject
  B  predicate
  C  neither

_____ 4. A shark has sharp <u>teeth</u>.
  A  subject
  B  predicate
  C  neither

_____ 5. <u>Mechanics</u> have many tools.
  A  subject
  B  predicate
  C  neither

_____ 6. Many robots <u>do</u> the work of humans.
  A  subject
  B  predicate
  C  neither

_____ 7. Restaurants <u>sell</u> food and drink.
  A  subject
  B  predicate
  C  neither

_____ 8. Some <u>daisies</u> grow along roadsides.
  A  subject
  B  predicate
  C  neither

_____ 9. Satellites circle the <u>earth</u>.
  A  subject
  B  predicate
  C  neither

_____ 10. The goldfish <u>swam</u> around in its bowl.
  A  subject
  B  predicate
  C  neither

_____ 11. The Panama Canal connects <u>two</u> oceans.
  A  subject
  B  predicate
  C  neither

_____ 12. Pinecones <u>contain</u> pine tree seeds.
  A  subject
  B  predicate
  C  neither

Name _____ Date _____

## CHAPTER 14  Complete Subjects

**[14B.1]** A **complete subject** includes all the words used to identify the person, place, thing, or idea that the sentence is about.

**EXERCISE** Write the complete subject of each sentence on the lines provided.

(1) Some flags signal a meaning. (2) A red flag means danger. (3) An upside-down flag means distress. (4) A white flag means surrender in battle.

(5) Every independent country flies its own flag. (6) Many countries show special symbols on their flags. (7) The Mexican flag pictures an eagle and a snake. (8) The Lebanese flag shows one of the famous cedars of Lebanon. (9) Each state in the United States flies its own flag. (10) Many private organizations have flags of their own. (11) Some important government offices have their own flags too.

1. _____
2. _____
3. _____
4. _____
5. _____
6. _____
7. _____
8. _____
9. _____
10. _____
11. _____

Name _____ Date _____

# CHAPTER 14 Simple Subjects

**[14B.2]** A **simple subject** is the main person, place, thing, or idea that the sentence is about.

**EXERCISE A** Identify the simple subject in each sentence.

_____ 1. The water in every ocean moves constantly.
   A ocean
   B water
   C moves

_____ 2. Earth's coasts change shape continually as a result.
   A shape
   B result
   C coasts

_____ 3. Huge waves pound at the edges of the continents.
   A pound
   B waves
   C continents

_____ 4. Ocean waves shift the land along the coasts.
   A waves
   B land
   C coasts

_____ 5. This constant motion carries away sand, dirt, and plants.
   A carries
   B motion
   C sand

_____ 6. Rocky shores resist this action.
   A Rocky
   B shores
   C action

**EXERCISE B** Underline the simple subject in each of the following sentences.

7. High sea cliffs form along such shores.

8. Soft, sandy beaches erode more easily.

9. Currents of water carve small inlets along sandy shores.

10. Some waves along the coast carry rocks and pebbles to shore.

11. The coasts of the world shift gradually over the years.

12. Around 44,000 storms occur each day on Earth.

13. A summer thunderstorm releases a huge amount of energy.

Name _____  Date _____

## CHAPTER 14  Complete Predicates

**[14C.1]** A **complete predicate** includes all the words that tell what the subject is doing or that tell something about the subject.

**EXERCISE A** Identify the complete predicate in each sentence.

_____ 1. Cinnamon adds a delicious taste to many foods.
   A  Cinnamon adds
   B  adds
   C  adds a delicious taste to many foods

_____ 2. The ancient Greeks used cinnamon in perfumes.
   A  used cinnamon in perfumes
   B  The ancient Greeks
   C  Greeks used cinnamon

_____ 3. The Romans flavored their food with it.
   A  The Romans
   B  Romans flavored
   C  flavored their food with it

_____ 4. The ancient Egyptians made medicine from cinnamon.
   A  made medicine from cinnamon
   B  The ancient Egyptians
   C  Egyptians made medicine

_____ 5. Some ancient people used cinnamon as money.
   A  Some ancient people
   B  people used cinnamon
   C  used cinnamon as money

_____ 6. Farmers remove the bark from cinnamon trees.
   A  Farmers remove
   B  remove the bark
   C  remove the bark from cinnamon trees

**EXERCISE B** Underline the complete predicate in each sentence of the paragraph below.

(7) Many icebergs near Greenland tower above the ocean. (8) Ocean currents sweep them out to sea. (9) Icebergs drift into the ship lanes in the North Atlantic. (10) Thick fog hides the icebergs in spring and summer. (11) A Coast Guard unit patrols during the iceberg season. (12) Navigators on board ships watch radar screens. (13) These sailors check the positions of icebergs. (14) Pilots drop buoys with radio transmitters onto icebergs. (15) The transmitters send signals to a satellite in space. (16) Scientists map the locations of the icebergs. (17) The patrol broadcasts this information to ship captains in the area.

Name _____  Date _____

# CHAPTER 14   Simple Predicates, or Verbs

**[14C.2]** A **simple predicate**, or **verb**, is the main word or phrase in the complete predicate.

**EXERCISE** On the blank, write the simple predicate in each sentence below.

_____ 1. Some birds live near human beings.

_____ 2. They build nests in trees and bushes near houses.

_____ 3. Birdhouses attract other birds to neighborhoods.

_____ 4. People see birds in parks and school yards.

_____ 5. These birds seek food in yards and gardens.

_____ 6. Many birds eat seeds and nuts.

_____ 7. Chickadees enjoy peanut butter.

_____ 8. Most birds fly to bird feeders in winter.

_____ 9. Different birdhouses suit different kinds of birds.

_____ 10. Many people watch for different kinds of birds in their yards.

_____ 11. Baby birds hatch in the late spring.

_____ 12. Birds build their nests out of sticks and twigs.

# CHAPTER 14  Complete and Simple Subjects and Predicates

**EXERCISE A** Underline the complete subject once and the simple subject twice in each of the following sentences.

1. Most large cities have parks and gardens.

2. The citizens of Fort Worth, Texas, have an unusual garden.

3. City workers cleared five entire city blocks.

4. A famous architect planned a garden for the area.

5. The entire garden is made up of displays of water.

6. Noisy, lively waterfalls dash over concrete walls.

7. Calm, quiet water flows in streams beside stairways.

**EXERCISE B** Underline the complete predicate once and the simple predicate twice in each of the following sentences.

8. The clock ticked loudly in the quiet room.

9. Tommy jumped up and down on the bed.

10. We all watched for shooting stars.

11. The boy in the last row answered the question correctly.

12. I made the strawberry jam in that jar myself.

13. Loud music blasted from the open window.

14. A small trout swims faster than a person.

# CHAPTER 14  Verb Phrases

**[14C.3]** The main verb and any helping verbs make up a **verb phrase**.

> **EXERCISE** Underline the verb phrase in each sentence below.

1. Ostriches <u>do have</u> the remains of wings.

2. Their wings <u>have become</u> useless for flight.

3. Most of these birds <u>will reach</u> a height of about eight feet.

4. Ostriches <u>can run</u> 25 miles per hour.

5. An ostrich's legs <u>will grow</u> long and powerful.

6. Their feet <u>do have</u> only two toes.

7. One ostrich egg <u>can weigh</u> as much as 24 chicken eggs.

8. People <u>would pluck</u> male ostrich feathers for their beauty.

9. They <u>would use</u> these plumes as decorations on hats and dresses.

10. Huge ostrich farms <u>were located</u> in South Africa and Australia.

11. The demand for ostrich feathers <u>has passed</u>.

12. Artificial feathers <u>have replaced</u> real ostrich feathers.

# CHAPTER 14  Interrupted Verb Phrases

**EXERCISE** The verb phrase in each of the following sentences is interrupted by one or more words. In each sentence, underline the word or words that interrupt the verb phrase. Then write the verb phrase on the line provided.

_____  1. Our crops do not get enough water.

_____  2. Is the sun shining this morning?

_____  3. A sailplane does not make any noise.

_____  4. A driver should always come to a sudden stop here.

_____  5. Does the bus stop at this corner?

_____  6. Houseplants will seldom do well without sun.

_____  7. Will the baseball team practice this afternoon?

_____  8. The sun hasn't shone for ten days in a row.

_____  9. Hal can hardly lift that dog.

_____  10. Has the temperature gone below zero?

_____  11. Hail may sometimes be the size of golf balls.

_____  12. The sky will always look black in space.

Name _____ Date _____

# CHAPTER 14   Different Positions of Subjects

**[14D]** The subject of a sentence can appear in different positions or be understood.

**[14D.1]** When the subject appears before the verb, a sentence is said to be in natural order.

**[14D.2]** When the verb comes before the subject, the sentence is in inverted order.

> **EXERCISE** Write N if the sentence is in natural order or I if it is in inverted order.

_____ 1. People have built special houses in different climates.

_____ 2. In warm climates, the rooms surround an open space.

_____ 3. Through open windows on both sides will blow cool breezes.

_____ 4. In the open courtyard may be a fireplace.

_____ 5. For a cook, this arrangement is quite comfortable.

_____ 6. The shady path is the best spot.

_____ 7. Behind the walls of the house is a private area.

_____ 8. On the roofs are wind scoops.

_____ 9. Houses in cold climates might have fireplaces in every room.

_____ 10. In hot climates, people build houses with thick walls.

_____ 11. Was this a common design in olden days?

_____ 12. Near the fir slept the dachshund.

_____ 13. Roberta has operated this computer before.

_____ 14. Over the beam vaulted the gymnast.

_____ 15. There are some mittens in the chest.

_____ 16. Down the hill swooped the skier.

_____ 17. There are three pizzas for you at Tom's Pizza Shop on Elm Street.

Name _____    Date _____

# CHAPTER 14  Compound Subjects

**[14E.1]** A **compound subject** is two or more subjects in one sentence that have the same verb and are joined by a conjunction.

**EXERCISE A** Identify the compound subject in each sentence.

_____  1. Baseball and basketball are my favorite sports.
- A  favorite, sports
- B  Baseball, basketball
- C  basketball
- D  Baseball

_____  2. Sunny days and cool nights come in September.
- A  Sunny, cool
- B  nights, September
- C  days, nights
- D  days

_____  3. Oranges, lemons, and limes are citrus fruits.
- A  citrus, fruits
- B  lemons, limes
- C  Oranges, lemons
- D  Oranges, lemons, limes

_____  4. Henry or Jane is taking Spanish this term.
- A  Henry, Jane
- B  Jane, Spanish
- C  Henry, Spanish
- D  Spanish, term

_____  5. Tennis rackets and squash rackets are somewhat alike.
- A  Tennis, squash
- B  rackets, rackets
- C  squash, rackets
- D  rackets, alike

_____  6. Houseflies and mosquitoes are both harmful.
- A  mosquitoes, harmful
- B  Houseflies, both
- C  Houseflies, mosquitoes
- D  both, harmful

**EXERCISE B** Underline the compound subject in each of the following sentences.

7. A pool or an indoor track will be in the new gym.

8. Neil Armstrong and Buzz Aldrin made the first landing on the moon.

9. Violins and banjos both have strings.

10. Grass and bamboo are the same kind of plant.

11. Pictures and CDs are on loan in many libraries.

12. Is Rhode Island or Delaware the smallest state?

Name _____ Date _____

## CHAPTER 14 Compound Verbs

**[14E.2]** A **compound verb** is two or more verbs that have the same subject and are joined by a conjunction.

**EXERCISE A** Identify the compound verb in each sentence.

_____ 1. The spider has stung the moth and now is waiting.
   A  stung, moth
   B  spider, stung
   C  has stung, is waiting
   D  has stung

_____ 2. The eagle has caught the fish and is bringing it to the nest.
   A  has caught, is bringing
   B  caught, nest
   C  eagle, bringing
   D  nest, eagle

_____ 3. Pedro balanced on his head but fell twice.
   A  Pedro, balanced
   B  head, Pedro
   C  fell, twice
   D  balanced, fell

_____ 4. The coach blew the whistle and motioned to Mac.
   A  blew, whistle
   B  blew, motioned
   C  coach, blew
   D  Mac, coach

_____ 5. The goalie grabbed the ball and threw it toward me.
   A  ball, threw
   B  threw, me
   C  goalie, grabbed
   D  grabbed, threw

_____ 6. The driver stepped on the brake and stopped the car.
   A  driver, stepped
   B  stopped, car
   C  stepped, stopped
   D  car, stepped

**EXERCISE B** Underline the compound verb in each of the following sentences.

7. Estelle has bought a racket and is here on the court.

8. Our cat caught a mole, carried it home, and laid it on the doorstep.

9. Jack will pump gas or will test the tires.

10. On the moon, Neil Armstrong planted a flag and gathered some rocks.

11. Caleb brought the sandwiches but forgot the thermos.

12. Yolanda went home and finished her project.

# CHAPTER 14 — Kinds of Sentences

**[14F.1]** A **declarative sentence** makes a statement or expresses an opinion and ends with a period.
**[14F.2]** An **interrogative sentence** asks a question and ends with a question mark.
**[14F.3]** An **imperative sentence** makes a request or gives a command and ends with either a period or an exclamation point.
**[14F.4]** An **exclamatory sentence** expresses strong feeling and ends with an exclamation point.

> **EXERCISE** Identify each sentence below by writing *declarative*, *interrogative*, *imperative*, or *exclamatory* on the line provided.

1. Have you ever looked carefully at a spider's web?
2. Spiders build their webs indoors and outdoors.
3. Look carefully around your house or your yard.
4. Corners near the ceiling are good places for webs in the house.
5. What beautiful designs spiders make!
6. What is a spider's web made of?
7. Check bushes, hedges, and grass blades for outdoor webs.
8. A spider weaves its web from silk.
9. Why do so many spiders build webs?
10. Spiders catch their meals in their webs.
11. What a clever idea that is!
12. Spiders just wait quietly in the web.
13. Sooner or later a bug will land on it.
14. Watch a spider wrap its catch in silk.

Name _____   Date _____

# CHAPTER 14   The Sentence Review

**EXERCISE** Identify the term that correctly describes the underlined word or words.

_____ 1. <u>Sylvia</u> and <u>John</u> won first place in the dance contest.
   A  complete subject
   B  compound subject
   C  simple subject
   D  inverted order

_____ 2. Baxter <u>might want</u> those leftovers.
   A  compound predicate
   B  simple predicate
   C  complete predicate
   D  verb phrase

_____ 3. <u>Minor earthquakes</u> occur in California almost every day.
   A  compound verb
   B  complete subject
   C  verb phrase
   D  simple subject

_____ 4. <u>Please take your muddy shoes off when you come in the house.</u>
   A  exclamatory sentence
   B  declarative sentence
   C  imperative sentence
   D  interrogative sentence

_____ 5. Monica <u>brought</u> her textbook but <u>forgot</u> her essay that was due today.
   A  compound verb
   B  simple predicate
   C  verb phrase
   D  complete predicate

_____ 6. <u>Here are the groceries you wanted.</u>
   A  interrogative sentence
   B  inverted order
   C  imperative sentence
   D  natural order

_____ 7. In ancient times, salt and pepper <u>were very expensive and rare spices</u>.
   A  verb phrase
   B  compound verb
   C  complete predicate
   D  simple predicate

_____ 8. <u>Trying to practice for the audition.</u>
   A  declarative sentence
   B  inverted order
   C  complete subject
   D  sentence fragment

_____ 9. <u>I can't decide whether I want to order pasta or pizza.</u>
   A  imperative sentence
   B  sentence fragment
   C  natural order
   D  exclamatory sentence

_____ 10. My third-floor <u>bedroom</u> has a fresh coat of blue paint.
   A  simple subject
   B  compound subject
   C  simple predicate
   D  complete predicate

Name _____   Date _____

# CHAPTER 15  Nouns

**[15A]** A **noun** is a word that names a person, a place, a thing, or an idea.

> **EXERCISE** Write the nouns from each sentence on the lines provided.

1. Loyalty and honesty are important qualities in a friend.
   _____

2. The stars and moon appeared in the night sky.
   _____

3. The truck moved slowly down the avenue.
   _____

4. A bug landed on the patio.
   _____

5. Chairs and instruments were placed on the stage.
   _____

6. The beach is at the edge of the sea as well as the land.
   _____

7. Animals such as clams, snails, and gulls feed and live along the shore.
   _____

8. The beauty and mystery of the ocean attract people too.
   _____

9. The tide floods the marshes near the beach twice a day.
   _____

10. Millions of creatures begin life in such spots.
    _____

11. For this reason, marshes are called cradles or nurseries of the sea.
    _____

Name _____  Date _____

### CHAPTER 15  Compound Nouns

**[15A2]** A noun that includes more than one word is called a **compound noun**.

> **EXERCISE** Use a dictionary to decide if the underlined words are spelled correctly. Write C for correct or I for incorrect.

_____ 1. My great grandmother is very old.

_____ 2. At dinner, they cooked over the camp-fire.

_____ 3. Let me see your new cellphone.

_____ 4. My father bought a new DVD player.

_____ 5. My sister likes to play on the play-ground.

_____ 6. We always have dinner in the diningroom.

_____ 7. Did you find the bath room?

_____ 8. We hiked all day through the foot hills.

_____ 9. After the storm, we saw a rainbow.

_____ 10. The sunset was beautiful.

_____ 11. The jet-stream often determines our weather.

_____ 12. A policeofficer has a very difficult job.

_____ 13. My brother likes to throw snow-balls in the winter.

_____ 14. The player hit a home run.

_____ 15. Do you think we will ever build a spacestation?

_____ 16. The early space craft often crashed.

_____ 17. I found only one meat-ball in my spaghetti.

_____ 18. My mother planted a rose bush.

_____ 19. The earthquake was very destructive.

_____ 20. Everyone in town looks forward to the county fair.

# CHAPTER 15  Common and Proper Nouns

**[15A.3]** A **common noun** names any person, place, or thing. A **proper noun** names a particular person, place, or thing.

**EXERCISE** Write the underlined nouns from the paragraph below in the appropriate column of the chart.

Jumbo was the name of a famous elephant. Jumbo was captured in Africa and shipped to England. His new home became the London Zoological Gardens. The English admired the size and dignity of the great elephant. The children of London rode on his back. After a few years, Jumbo was sold to P.T. Barnum. Barnum was the owner of a circus in the United States. The people of England, including Queen Victoria, protested the sale. Jumbo sailed across the Atlantic Ocean on schedule. The ship landed at the docks in New York City. Jumbo joined the circus and became a famous attraction.

| Common Nouns | Proper Nouns |
| --- | --- |
|  |  |
|  |  |
|  |  |
|  |  |
|  |  |
|  |  |
|  |  |
|  |  |
|  |  |
|  |  |
|  |  |
|  |  |
|  |  |
|  |  |
|  |  |

Name _____   Date _____

## CHAPTER 15  Pronoun Antecedents

**[15B]** A **pronoun** is a word that takes the place of one or more nouns.
**[15B.1]** The noun that a pronoun replaces, or refers to, is called its **antecedent**.

> **EXERCISE** Underline the pronoun in each sentence. Then draw an arrow to the pronoun's antecedent.

1. Mom told Brian to help her.

2. My cousin and I built our first snow fort.

3. Sharon picked up the cat and petted it.

4. Danny baked a beautiful cake. He saved the horrible dinner.

5. Susan made her prettiest dress this year.

6. Ruth said she wanted to go to the parade.

7. The Murphys are selling their boat.

8. Cameron can't find his library book.

9. The children can't find their mittens.

10. Tom said he didn't want to go to the movie.

11. Judy finished her book before the end of the week.

12. Dr. Roberto said that the snake shed its skin.

13. Shawna is giving a birthday party for her best friend.

14. Mom and Dad packed their bags for the trip.

15. Brent gave his report yesterday.

## CHAPTER 15  Personal Pronouns

**EXERCISE A** Choose the answer that identifies the personal pronouns in each sentence.

_____ 1. I will speak to him about your assignment.
   A  I, him
   B  I, him, your
   C  I, will, him
   D  I, your

_____ 2. We gave their presents to them at suppertime.
   A  We, their, them
   B  We, their
   C  their, them
   D  We, gave, their

_____ 3. He and I sent her a card from Pennsylvania.
   A  He, I
   B  He
   C  I, her
   D  He, I, her

_____ 4. The blue gloves are yours, and the green gloves are mine.
   A  yours
   B  yours, mine
   C  gloves, yours, mine
   D  mine

_____ 5. She lifted the tray and handed it to me.
   A  She, tray
   B  She, me
   C  tray, me
   D  She, it, me

_____ 6. You can offer him a ride in our car.
   A  You, him, our
   B  You, him, car
   C  You, him
   D  him, our

**EXERCISE B** Underline the personal pronouns in each sentence.

7. Will they present their skit at the assembly tomorrow?

8. Phil picked up my books and handed them to me.

9. Are the blue tickets theirs or ours?

10. His speech was a big surprise to us.

11. She invited us to their house for dinner.

12. I have my luggage with me.

13. We left our luggage at the cottage.

Name _____ Date _____

# CHAPTER 15  Reflexive and Intensive Pronouns

**[15B.3] Reflexive** and **intensive pronouns** refer to or emphasize a noun or another pronoun.

---

**EXERCISE A** Choose the correct reflexive or intensive pronoun for each sentence.

_____ 1. Lucinda and I are trying to teach _____ to swim the backstroke.
   A  ourselves
   B  myself
   C  herself

_____ 2. Kids, if you would keep _____ quiet for a minute, I could collect my thoughts!
   A  ourselves
   B  themselves
   C  yourselves

_____ 3. In my dream, a strange-looking beast was sunning _____ on a large purple rock.
   A  myself
   B  itself
   C  themselves

_____ 4. I _____ have no idea what you mean.
   A  yourself
   B  ourselves
   C  myself

_____ 5. After three months of trying, Carlos finally taught _____ to stop cracking his knuckles.
   A  ourselves
   B  himself
   C  hisself

_____ 6. Even the members of the band _____ decided that their newest album wasn't as good as the last one.
   A  themselves
   B  himself
   C  theirselves

---

**EXERCISE B** Underline the reflexive or intensive pronoun in each sentence. Then write R if the pronoun is reflexive or I if it is intensive.

_____ 7. The poodle kept splashing itself and its puppies with the cold water from the pond.

_____ 8. After a few hours, Rick had persuaded himself that bungee jumping wasn't all that bad.

_____ 9. The tuba players themselves are getting tired of playing that song.

_____ 10. Mrs. Nolan had already committed herself to the project, but she was hoping for a little help from us.

_____ 11. The park ranger herself put out the forest fire before it spread.

_____ 12. I decided to help myself to an extra piece of cake.

_____ 13. Give yourselves a hand for your excellent work!

Name _____   Date _____

# CHAPTER 15  Other Kinds of Pronouns

**[15B.4] Indefinite pronouns** refer to unnamed people, places, things, or ideas.
**[15B.5] Demonstrative pronouns** point out a specific person, place, thing, or idea.
**[15B.6] Interrogative pronouns** are used to ask questions.

**EXERCISE A** Identify each underlined pronoun as indefinite, demonstrative, or interrogative.

_____ 1. Everybody enjoys a good laugh now and then.
   A indefinite
   B demonstrative
   C interrogative

_____ 2. That is a very strange story.
   A indefinite
   B demonstrative
   C interrogative

_____ 3. What is the name of a famous home run hitter?
   A indefinite
   B demonstrative
   C interrogative

_____ 4. The chef cut all of the vegetables into small pieces.
   A indefinite
   B demonstrative
   C interrogative

_____ 5. Because of the storm, none of the planes arrived on schedule.
   A indefinite
   B demonstrative
   C interrogative

_____ 6. Which is the best card for the occasion?
   A indefinite
   B demonstrative
   C interrogative

**EXERCISE B** Underline the pronoun in each sentence below. Then identify the pronoun by writing *indefinite*, *demonstrative*, or *interrogative* on the line provided.

_____  7. Sandy left these on the table in the front room.

_____  8. Tom has starred in several of the school plays.

_____  9. Who is the best candidate for mayor of the city?

_____ 10. Both of the coaches spoke at the pep rally last night.

_____ 11. This is the last empty seat in the theater.

_____ 12. Most of the crew members were on board during the storm.

Name _____ Date _____

# CHAPTER 15 Nouns and Pronouns Review

**EXERCISE** Identify each underlined word or group of words in the paragraphs below.

(1) Ellen and her twin brother, David, decided to make a diorama about the (2) seashore for their science project. Ellen (3) herself already had a large collection of seashells that (4) they could use. David went to Lakeland Aquarium on (5) Main Street and bought a large bag of (6) sand to make the base. They used cardboard for the bottom, the back, and the sides.

(7) Both were very happy with how their project turned out. (8) "This looks great!" said Ellen. (9) "What do you think, David?"

"I think we make an excellent team!" (10) he said.

_____ 1. A common noun
B proper noun
C personal pronoun
D intensive pronoun

_____ 2. A proper noun
B indefinite pronoun
C compound noun
D reflexive pronoun

_____ 3. A demonstrative pronoun
B reflexive pronoun
C common noun
D intensive pronoun

_____ 4. A personal pronoun
B interrogative pronoun
C demonstrative pronoun
D reflexive pronoun

_____ 5. A compound noun
B proper noun
C common noun
D indefinite pronoun

_____ 6. A proper noun
B pronoun antecedent
C common noun
D compound noun

_____ 7. A reflexive pronoun
B intensive pronoun
C personal pronoun
D indefinite pronoun

_____ 8. A demonstrative pronoun
B reflexive pronoun
C intensive pronoun
D personal pronoun

_____ 9. A interrogative pronoun
B personal pronoun
C indefinite pronoun
D reflexive pronoun

_____ 10. A common noun
B personal pronoun
C pronoun antecedent
D indefinite pronoun

Name _____ Date _____

# CHAPTER 16  Action Verbs

**[16A]** A **verb** is a word used to express action or a state of being.
**[16A.1]** An **action verb** tells what action a subject is performing.

---

**EXERCISE A** Identify the action verb in each sentence

_____ 1. Carl pitched the first game.
  A  Carl
  B  first
  C  pitched
  D  game

_____ 2. The large vase tipped over.
  A  large
  B  tipped
  C  over
  D  vase

_____ 3. Belinda always thinks positively.
  A  positively
  B  always
  C  Belinda
  D  thinks

_____ 4. We believed her story.
  A  believed
  B  We
  C  her
  D  story

_____ 5. The Fishers own a canoe.
  A  Fishers
  B  own
  C  The
  D  canoe

_____ 6. With a wide grin, Dad placed the huge fish on the table.
  A  wide
  B  huge
  C  placed
  D  Dad

---

**EXERCISE B** Underline the action verb in each of the following sentences.

7. Phil dodged the tackle.

8. A comet's tail always points away from the sun.

9. The swimmer dived from the dock at the end of the lawn into the clear lake.

10. Everyone hoped for sunny days.

11. Last summer, I visited my grandparents in Idaho for three weeks.

12. The telephone rang all morning.

13. The sailboat skimmed across the bay.

# CHAPTER 16 Action Verbs

**EXERCISE** List all the action verbs in this paragraph.

People made vinegar thousands of years ago. Ancient Babylonians cooked with it. The first great doctor, Hippocrates, prescribed it. Roman legionnaires used it as a beverage. Today, campers treat rashes and bites with it. It also helps with sunburn and bruises. Pickle makers use thousands of gallons of it every year. People make vinegar from many kinds of fruits and vegetables. After a shampoo, some people rinse their hair with vinegar and water. People keep vinegar in their kitchens and their workshops. It removes stains and odors from pots and pans. It absorbs the smell of fresh paint. It keeps windshields free of frost. It takes stubborn decals off glass and paint. Vinegar cleans windows well too.

Name _____  Date _____

## CHAPTER 16  Transitive and Intransitive Verbs

**[16B]** A **transitive verb** expresses action directly toward a person or a thing. An **intransitive verb** expresses action that is not directed at a person or a thing.

> **EXERCISE** Write T if the underlined verb is transitive or I if it is intransitive.

_____ 1. The teacher <u>chose</u> six ushers for the play.

_____ 2. The ushers <u>dressed</u> neatly.

_____ 3. The ant <u>crawls</u> at the rate of twelve feet per minute.

_____ 4. Toni <u>smelled</u> the perfume.

_____ 5. Today Ronnie <u>tasted</u> clams for the first time.

_____ 6. At the store, Mom <u>bought</u> milk and eggs.

_____ 7. Five minutes later, Paul <u>remembered</u> the answer.

_____ 8. Thomas Edison <u>invented</u> wax paper.

_____ 9. We <u>ate</u> before the play.

_____ 10. Camels <u>carry</u> riders across the desert.

_____ 11. The seals <u>played</u> in the surf.

_____ 12. Last week, we <u>hiked</u> the steepest trail.

_____ 13. The couple <u>strolled</u> along the busy street.

_____ 14. Magellan <u>began</u> his trip around the word in 1519.

_____ 15. I <u>smell</u> smoke!

_____ 16. Jayden <u>waved</u> to her friend.

_____ 17. Tony <u>felt</u> the pony's side.

_____ 18. Benjamin Franklin <u>founded</u> the world's first lending library.

Name _____ Date _____

# CHAPTER 16 Helping Verbs

**[16C]** A **helping verb**, or auxiliary verb, is a verb that is combined with a main verb to form a verb phrase.

**[16C.1]** A **verb phrase** is made up of a main verb and one or more helping verbs.

**EXERCISE A** Identify the verb phrase in each sentence.

_____ 1. My brother has been watching tennis games on TV.
    **A** has
    **B** has been watching
    **C** been watching
    **D** watching tennis

_____ 2. Five robins are looking for worms on our lawn.
    **A** are looking
    **B** are
    **C** looking for
    **D** for worms

_____ 3. Many elm trees have been killed in this country.
    **A** trees have
    **B** been
    **C** been killed
    **D** have been killed

_____ 4. Jill was watering the plants in the window boxes.
    **A** Jill was
    **B** watering the
    **C** was watering
    **D** was

_____ 5. Patty and I have been waiting an hour for you.
    **A** have
    **B** have been
    **C** waiting
    **D** have been waiting

_____ 6. Joe has been listening to music through his headphones.
    **A** through
    **B** has been
    **C** has been listening
    **D** listening to music

**EXERCISE B** Underline the verb phrase in each sentence. On the blank, write the helping verb.

_____ 7. You should have seen the golden carp in that pool.

_____ 8. Ginny will spot you by your red scarf.

_____ 9. You must be home by nine tonight at the very latest.

_____ 10. Emily might have gone instead of me.

_____ 11. We would have felt better with smaller dinner portions.

_____ 12. I haven't yet bought a ticket to the football game.

# CHAPTER 16  Linking Verbs

**[16D]** A **linking verb** links the subject with another word that renames or describes the subject.

**EXERCISE A** Identify the linking verb in each sentence.

_____ 1. Live oak trees are green year-round.
   A green
   B are
   C year
   D Live

_____ 2. The park is full of fantastic attractions.
   A is
   B full
   C of
   D fantastic

_____ 3. Her photographs were beautiful.
   A her
   B photographs
   C were
   D beautiful

_____ 4. Your voice sounds scratchy.
   A your
   B voice
   C sounds
   D scratchy

_____ 5. That dog must be very old by now.
   A dog
   B must be
   C be very
   D very old

_____ 6. The small children grew restless during the performance.
   A small
   B restless
   C during
   D grew

**EXERCISE B** Underline the linking verb in each sentence.

7. Could this rumor be true?

8. The comedian might have been funnier.

9. Those tennis shoes were too small.

10. Our center is the tallest person in school.

11. It was too early for ripe blackberries.

12. Those trees are pines.

13. This amount will be enough for me.

Name _____ Date _____

# CHAPTER 16 — Linking Verbs

> **EXERCISE** Underline the linking verbs in the following sentences. Then circle the words that the verb links.

1. She has been the champion for three years in a row.
2. Should Alan have been the speaker at graduation?
3. Last night's sunset was bright red.
4. The weather for the race could not be better.
5. This watermelon tastes sweeter today.
6. The other team grew stronger in the second half.
7. Were the old shoes more comfortable for you?
8. The air seems much cooler in the shade.
9. The rain will be heavy tomorrow.
10. Eric and Rosa are members of the soccer team.
11. Laura has been a pianist for many years.
12. The azaleas turned brown after the freeze.
13. A snake's skin is quite dry.
14. They are the winners of the race.
15. You might be right.

Name _____  Date _____

# CHAPTER 16  Linking Verb or Action Verb?

**EXERCISE** Decide whether the verb in each sentence is a linking verb or an action verb.

_____ 1. Evan <u>looked</u> everywhere for his baseball cap.
   A  linking verb
   B  action verb

_____ 2. Jack <u>looked</u> better after his long night's sleep.
   A  linking verb
   B  action verb

_____ 3. Now the thunder <u>sounds</u> louder.
   A  linking verb
   B  action verb

_____ 4. Hazel <u>tasted</u> the pizza cautiously.
   A  linking verb
   B  action verb

_____ 5. This Persian cat's fur <u>feels</u> very soft.
   A  linking verb
   B  action verb

_____ 6. Yesterday the class <u>seemed</u> short.
   A  linking verb
   B  action verb

_____ 7. Mexican pepper sauce <u>tastes</u> really spicy.
   A  linking verb
   B  action verb

_____ 8. All of us <u>smelled</u> the roses.
   A  linking verb
   B  action verb

_____ 9. Savannah <u>felt</u> raindrops on her head.
   A  linking verb
   B  action verb

_____ 10. Julia <u>stayed</u> in her room during the television program.
   A  linking verb
   B  action verb

_____ 11. <u>Did</u> you <u>become</u> restless during the last lecture?
   A  linking verb
   B  action verb

_____ 12. That bell <u>sounded</u> the end of the first class.
   A  linking verb
   B  action verb

Name _____  Date _____

## CHAPTER 16 — Linking Verb or Action Verb?

**EXERCISE** Underline the verb in each sentence. Then write L if it's a linking verb or A if it's an action verb.

_____ 1. The audience remained quiet.

_____ 2. I feel absolutely great today.

_____ 3. The bugle sounded the beginning of the race.

_____ 4. The cupcakes smelled delightful.

_____ 5. She turned the doorknob.

_____ 6. Did you smell this perfume?

_____ 7. It became the town's first skateboarding park.

_____ 8. The vegetables taste great.

_____ 9. The oranges looked delicious.

_____ 10. My dog appeared in the doorway.

_____ 11. I became thirsty after the run.

_____ 12. Did you look for your jacket in the closet?

_____ 13. We tasted the strawberries from the store.

_____ 14. The girl seemed ill before class.

_____ 15. The dog grew three feet high.

_____ 16. The man remained on the stage.

# CHAPTER 16  Verbs Review

**EXERCISE** Identify the term that correctly describes the underlined word or words.

_____ 1. Yesterday, Armin <u>visited</u> the department store.
  A  linking verb
  B  transitive verb
  C  intransitive verb
  D  helping verb

_____ 2. Emily and I <u>have been waiting</u> for this concert.
  A  verb phrase
  B  linking verb
  C  helping verb
  D  transitive verb

_____ 3. That vegetable soup <u>smells</u> delicious!
  A  action verb
  B  helping verb
  C  transitive verb
  D  linking verb

_____ 4. Lucy <u>looked</u> at the shoe display.
  A  helping verb
  B  transitive verb
  C  linking verb
  D  intransitive verb

_____ 5. Ben <u>was</u> worn out after studying all day at the library.
  A  helping verb
  B  linking verb
  C  action verb
  D  transitive verb

_____ 6. Ted <u>could</u> be the school high-jump champion this year.
  A  linking verb
  B  helping verb
  C  intransitive verb
  D  transitive verb

_____ 7. <u>Are</u> some sharks as big as whales?
  A  intransitive verb
  B  transitive verb
  C  linking verb
  D  helping verb

_____ 8. Tamara <u>walked</u> to a nearby park.
  A  intransitive verb
  B  transitive verb
  C  helping verb
  D  linking verb

_____ 9. Marlon <u>was watering</u> the plants every day.
  A  linking verb
  B  helping verb
  C  verb phrase
  D  intransitive verb

_____ 10. The crowd <u>remained</u> near the door.
  A  transitive verb
  B  intransitive verb
  C  helping verb
  D  linking verb

Name _____ Date _____

# CHAPTER 17  Adjectives

**[17A]** An **adjective** is a word that modifies a noun or pronoun.

**EXERCISE A** Identify the adjective or adjectives that modify the underlined word in each sentence.

_____ 1. Pioneer farmers settled the rich <u>farmland</u> of the Midwest.
  A  Pioneer
  B  rich
  C  farmers

_____ 2. Rocks and trees did not exist in the fertile, grassy <u>soil</u>.
  A  fertile, grassy
  B  Rocks, grassy
  C  Rocks, trees

_____ 3. The pioneers built small <u>homes</u> of thick sod.
  A  built
  B  thick
  C  small

_____ 4. These houses protected the pioneers from hot and cold <u>weather</u>.
  A  These, houses
  B  houses, pioneers
  C  hot, cold

_____ 5. With simple plows they turned over long <u>rows</u> of sod.
  A  sod
  B  long
  C  turned

_____ 6. The earth was tough with deep <u>roots</u> of grasses.
  A  deep
  B  grasses
  C  tough

**EXERCISE B** Underline the adjectives in the following sentences. Then draw an arrow to the word each adjective modifies.

7. These walls used to be covered with purple wallpaper.

8. Strong winds come from opposite directions and smash together.

9. Wild storms can cause much damage.

10. Twenty red and green balloons floated above.

11. Those houses were occupied for more than seventy years.

12. Famous actors often live in enormous homes.

# CHAPTER 17  Different Positions of Adjectives

**EXERCISE** Circle the noun modified by the underlined adjective or adjectives in each sentence.

1. The batter, <u>confident</u>, grinned at the pitcher.
2. The <u>heavy</u> rainfall did little to ease the drought.
3. The cat was <u>happy</u> and <u>sleepy</u>.
4. The sun was <u>hot</u>.
5. Kerry bought <u>two</u> tickets.
6. The tree, <u>barren</u> and <u>dead</u>, drooped beneath the clouds.
7. Sid's <u>baseball</u> team won the championship.
8. The <u>red</u> flower is a zinnia.
9. <u>Six</u> weeks is enough time for rehearsal.
10. <u>Several</u> students wanted to play the lead role.
11. A <u>brown</u>, <u>spiny</u> monster was the star of the movie.
12. Sandra's <u>favorite</u> book is *Sarah, Plain and Tall*.
13. The meatloaf was <u>tender</u> and <u>juicy</u>.
14. The ball was rather <u>large</u>.

# CHAPTER 17  Proper Adjectives

**EXERCISE** Write the proper adjective in each sentence on the line provided.

_____  1. Bob wanted an English sheepdog for the longest time.

_____  2. I love to eat Chinese food.

_____  3. Barbara's Siamese cat has a bad temper.

_____  4. Samantha visited several African countries on her last vacation.

_____  5. A Congressional committee was formed to study the issue.

_____  6. Nick enjoys the Italian cookies his grandmother bakes.

_____  7. We could see the Mexican coast from the boat.

_____  8. Can you name the Canadian provinces?

_____  9. My neighbor was a delegate to the last Republican convention.

_____  10. My sister loves the old German forests.

_____  11. Greek food is very healthy.

_____  12. They enjoy Hawaiian sunsets.

_____  13. The French poodle won the dog show.

_____  14. The British ship sailed past.

_____  15. My aunt is the Democratic candidate for county commissioner.

_____  16. I really prefer Indian music.

_____  17. American horses are descended from mustangs.

_____  18. The Irish soccer team won the tournament.

# CHAPTER 17  Adjective, Noun, or Pronoun?

**EXERCISE** Decide whether the underlined word in each sentence is used as an adjective, noun, or pronoun.

_____ 1. The Kellys built a tree house in their <u>big</u> oak.
  A adjective
  B noun
  C pronoun

_____ 2. <u>Many</u> attempt that climb, but few reach the top.
  A adjective
  B noun
  C pronoun

_____ 3. Marilyn has become a <u>star</u> actress.
  A adjective
  B noun
  C pronoun

_____ 4. Warren has made the first <u>team</u> at last.
  A adjective
  B noun
  C pronoun

_____ 5. <u>These</u> cassettes are very expensive.
  A adjective
  B noun
  C pronoun

_____ 6. During the ceremony, <u>each</u> of the players was introduced.
  A adjective
  B noun
  C pronoun

_____ 7. One of the greatest tennis players is a <u>Swiss</u>.
  A adjective
  B noun
  C pronoun

_____ 8. A planet is not a <u>star</u>.
  A adjective
  B noun
  C pronoun

_____ 9. Her favorite dessert is <u>apple</u> slices.
  A adjective
  B noun
  C pronoun

_____ 10. <u>Each</u> person will say a few words.
  A adjective
  B noun
  C pronoun

_____ 11. Barb certainly is a <u>team</u> player.
  A adjective
  B noun
  C pronoun

_____ 12. Well, <u>these</u> are my reasons for not going to that movie.
  A adjective
  B noun
  C pronoun

# CHAPTER 17 Adjective, Noun, or Pronoun?

**EXERCISE** Above each underlined word, write A for adjective, N for noun, or P for pronoun.

1. Which song did you choose?

2. We had to buy many gallons of paint.

3. I will need a new winter coat this year.

4. The baseball soared into the far bleachers.

5. That dog belongs to my best friend.

6. Many left the game early.

7. Finding enough time to study is a major problem for me.

8. That is Morgan's stamp collection.

9. Can the paint stains be removed from those rugs?

10. Ken has seen the movie several times already this week.

11. Those should be stored in the hall closet.

12. Last winter, we had twenty inches of snow.

| Name | Date |
|---|---|

# CHAPTER 17  Adverbs

**[17B]** An **adverb** is a word that modifies a verb, an adjective, or another adverb.

**EXERCISE A** Select the adverb that modifies the underlined word or words in each sentence.

_____ 1. Some people <u>travel</u> south to Florida for the winter.
   A Some
   B people
   C south

_____ 2. Some animals <u>sleep</u> deeply all winter.
   A deeply
   B all
   C Some

_____ 3. Those animals easily <u>escape</u> harsh winters.
   A Those
   B harsh
   C easily

_____ 4. People usually <u>stay</u> at home during the winter.
   A during
   B usually
   C People

_____ 5. Most animals <u>do</u> not <u>sleep</u> all winter.
   A not
   B all
   C Most

_____ 6. The deep sleepers <u>are</u> scientifically <u>called</u> true hibernators.
   A true
   B scientifically
   C deep

**EXERCISE B** Underline the adverbs in the following sentences.

7. Groundhogs greedily eat huge amounts of food in the fall.

8. They slowly creep into their underground burrows.

9. During the winter, they sleep soundly.

10. Chickadees arrive at our feeder early in the morning.

11. The plane zoomed swiftly over the city.

12. Linda skied haphazardly between the trees.

13. The high wind fiercely blew the elm trees.

# CHAPTER 17 Adverbs

**EXERCISE** In the following sentences, find each adverb and the word or words it modifies. Then write them in the proper column of the chart.

1. Stand near the door to the classroom.
2. The big bear growled ferociously at the small bear.
3. I was floating in the pool calmly until now.
4. Finally, the last runner crossed the finish line.
5. The campers put their campfire out.
6. Rafe stopped at the corner and looked around.
7. Think carefully before you answer.
8. The old fence fell down.
9. Then the phone rang.
10. The council meeting ended abruptly.

| Adverb | Word(s) It Modifies |
|---|---|
| 1. | |
| 2. | |
| 3. | |
| 4. | |
| 5. | |
| 6. | |
| 7. | |
| 8. | |
| 9. | |
| 10. | |

# CHAPTER 17  Adverbs That Modify Verbs

**EXERCISE**  Write the adverb or adverbs that modify each underlined verb.

_____  1. The balloon <u>floated</u> up.

_____  2. Then she <u>sighed</u>.

_____  3. The car <u>stopped</u> suddenly.

_____  4. Summer nearly <u>won</u> the contest.

_____  5. James <u>packed</u> his clothes neatly.

_____  6. Soon we <u>will be leaving</u> for vacation.

_____  7. Dad <u>has</u> not <u>visited</u> the Grand Canyon.

_____  8. <u>Does</u> the road frequently <u>curve</u>?

_____  9. Nervous people rarely <u>sit</u>.

_____  10. The huge crowd <u>rushed</u> forward.

_____  11. Lately, I <u>have been watching</u> the evening news.

_____  12. You really <u>forgot</u> the test?

_____  13. Suddenly, the sea <u>grew</u> dark.

_____  14. The band <u>is practicing</u> again.

_____  15. We <u>have traveled</u> everywhere in search of the perfect hamburger.

_____  16. A hard-boiled egg <u>will spin</u> easily.

_____  17. Cecily <u>will</u> never <u>go</u> on that ride.

_____  18. Don't <u>look</u> down at the ground!

# CHAPTER 17 — Adverbs That Modify Adjectives and Other Adverbs

**EXERCISE A** Select the adverb that modifies the underlined adjective or adverb in each sentence.

_____ 1. Pedro's compliments were truly <u>sincere</u>.
   A  were
   B  truly
   C  compliments

_____ 2. Ada finished her homework very <u>quickly</u>.
   A  very
   B  finished
   C  homework

_____ 3. Ken rode too <u>fast</u> around the bicycle track.
   A  around
   B  fast
   C  too

_____ 4. The actors were extremely <u>nervous</u>.
   A  actors
   B  extremely
   C  were

_____ 5. You should drive extra <u>carefully</u>.
   A  should
   B  drive
   C  extra

_____ 6. It rains quite <u>often</u> during the month of April.
   A  quite
   B  during
   C  month

**EXERCISE B** Rewrite the following sentences, adding an adverb to modify the underlined adjective or adverb.

7. Your turkey dinner tasted <u>delicious</u>.

_____

8. Jenni is <u>absent</u> from practice.

_____

9. Snow fell <u>heavily</u> for an hour.

_____

10. Robbie arrived <u>early</u> for the party.

_____

11. The truck was moving <u>slowly</u>.

_____

# CHAPTER 17  Adjectives and Adverbs Review

**EXERCISE** Write the letter of the term that correctly identifies the underlined word in each sentence.

_____ 1. Addison performed very well at <u>the</u> talent show.
  A  pronoun
  B  adverb
  C  proper adjective
  D  article

_____ 2. We have lived <u>here</u> since I was three years old.
  A  adjective
  B  adverb
  C  pronoun
  D  noun

_____ 3. I haven't known her very <u>long</u>.
  A  adjective
  B  pronoun
  C  proper adjective
  D  adverb

_____ 4. There were <u>long</u> lines at the grocery store.
  A  pronoun
  B  article
  C  adjective
  D  adverb

_____ 5. <u>That</u> is a slow train!
  A  pronoun
  B  adjective
  C  proper adjective
  D  adverb

_____ 6. Harris ran <u>fast</u> toward the finish line.
  A  pronoun
  B  adverb
  C  adjective
  D  noun

_____ 7. We ate in a <u>Japanese</u> restaurant last night.
  A  article
  B  proper noun
  C  proper adjective
  D  adverb

_____ 8. We are fighting for a <u>just</u> cause.
  A  adjective
  B  adverb
  C  pronoun
  D  article

_____ 9. Soon-Yi <u>just</u> got a new winter coat.
  A  pronoun
  B  proper adjective
  C  adjective
  D  adverb

_____ 10. It was <u>still</u> raining when I got to school.
  A  pronoun
  B  adverb
  C  adjective
  D  article

_____ 11. I bought ten DVDs at <u>a</u> garage sale.
  A  adjective
  B  adverb
  C  article
  D  pronoun

_____ 12. Dalen is trying out for the <u>basketball</u> team tomorrow.
  A  adjective
  B  pronoun
  C  noun
  D  adverb

Name _____  Date _____

## CHAPTER 18  Prepositions

**[18A]** A **preposition** is a word that shows the relationship between a noun or a pronoun and another word in the sentence.

---

**EXERCISE A** Select the preposition in each sentence.

_____ 1. The bear rolled off the log.
   A  off
   B  bear
   C  rolled

_____ 2. A praying mantis climbed through the window.
   A  climbed
   B  window
   C  through

_____ 3. Seagulls fly in large flocks.
   A  large
   B  in
   C  flocks

_____ 4. Birds sing to each other.
   A  to
   B  each
   C  other

_____ 5. We drove over the old bridge.
   A  drove
   B  the
   C  over

_____ 6. Whales are found around the world.
   A  found
   B  around
   C  the

---

**EXERCISE B** Underline the preposition in each sentence.

7. The sun slid across the sky.

8. Some settlers moved toward the West.

9. Many clocks are fitted with a chime.

10. Near the island, two otters played.

11. The house on the corner is vacant.

12. Tim saw you under the oak tree.

13. The game ended after 10 P.M.

# CHAPTER 18  Prepositions

> **EXERCISE** Fill in each blank with an appropriate preposition. There may be more than one answer that makes sense.

1. The cricket jumped _____ the boy.

2. The road _____ the river is closed.

3. Please hand me the book _____ the table.

4. The cat was sleeping _____ the couch.

5. The tiny mouse ran _____ the closet door.

6. Marco and Oliver swam _____ the river.

7. The kids rode their bikes _____ the park.

8. I accidentally dropped my keys _____ the soup.

9. Michelle kicked the soccer ball _____ Naomi.

10. The dog looked _____ the bushes.

11. The bird flew _____ the open window.

12. The stunt man dived _____ the high rocks.

13. That quilt was made _____ Kathy.

14. This trail leads _____ the river.

15. Penguins have wings _____ flippers.

Name _____  Date _____

## CHAPTER 18  Prepositional Phrases

**[18A.1]** A **prepositional phrase** is a group of words made up of a preposition, its object, and any words that modify the object.

**EXERCISE A**  Write the prepositional phrase in each sentence.

_____  1. We often pick peaches in May.

_____  2. Lee came with us.

_____  3. Hang that lantern on the hook.

_____  4. Everyone except Marci liked the show.

_____  5. The tulips in our garden are very beautiful this year.

_____  6. Before breakfast, our dog retrieves the paper.

_____  7. Water that plant beside the patio.

_____  8. A lazy cat was lying across the bed.

_____  9. The dog searched for its bone.

_____  10. The boy jumped off the diving board.

**EXERCISE B**  Underline the prepositional phrase in each sentence. Then write a new sentence using the same prepositional phrase.

11. The roads were covered with ice.
    _____

12. The small green lizard ran between the rocks.
    _____

13. We ate dinner at the restaurant.
    _____

14. Jane found her glasses on the bookshelf.
    _____

15. The hawk dove toward the ground.
    _____

# CHAPTER 18  Preposition or Adverb?

**EXERCISE** Write P if the underlined word is a preposition or A if it is an adverb.

_____ 1. The dog rolled <u>over</u>.

_____ 2. Put the chicken <u>in</u> the oven.

_____ 3. Did you jump <u>across</u>?

_____ 4. The truck backed <u>over</u> the log.

_____ 5. The lid fell <u>off</u> the pot.

_____ 6. Push that button <u>in</u>.

_____ 7. The horses trotted <u>around</u> the ring.

_____ 8. Have you been here <u>before</u>?

_____ 9. Let's hide <u>behind</u> this tree.

_____ 10. Jill walked <u>inside</u> the cave.

_____ 11. The canary flew <u>through</u> the open window.

_____ 12. We practiced our formations <u>before</u> the parade.

_____ 13. Suddenly my hat flew <u>off</u>.

_____ 14. Please don't run <u>around</u>.

_____ 15. The deal has fallen <u>through</u>.

_____ 16. I cannot see <u>inside</u>.

_____ 17. We all went <u>inside</u> the house.

_____ 18. Climb <u>up</u>.

_____ 19. His quarter rolled <u>down</u> the aisle.

Name _____  Date _____

## CHAPTER 18 — Conjunctions and Interjections

**[18B]** A **conjunction** connects words or groups of words; an **interjection** shows strong feelings.

**[18B.2]** A **conjunctive adverb** is an adverb that acts as a conjunction connecting complete ideas.

---

**EXERCISE A** Decide whether the underlined word or words in each sentence is a conjunction, a conjunctive adverb, or an interjection.

_____ 1. <u>Wow</u>! That was the best pass of the game.
   A  conjunction
   B  conjunctive adverb
   C  interjection

_____ 2. Gabrielle <u>or</u> Iris will give the next report.
   A  conjunction
   B  conjunctive adverb
   C  interjection

_____ 3. Our team won the debate; <u>therefore</u>, we decided to celebrate at Vinny's Pizza.
   A  conjunction
   B  conjunctive adverb
   C  interjection

_____ 4. <u>Oh</u>, I forgot my homework!
   A  conjunction
   B  conjunctive adverb
   C  interjection

_____ 5. This species of plant is easy to care for; <u>furthermore</u>, it grows beautiful flowers in the spring.
   A  conjunction
   B  conjunctive adverb
   C  interjection

_____ 6. Jamal will <u>either</u> fry <u>or</u> boil the potatoes.
   A  conjunction
   B  conjunctive adverb
   C  interjection

---

**EXERCISE B** Underline the conjunction, conjunctive adverb, or interjection in each sentence. Then identify the underlined word by writing C for conjunction, CA for conjunctive adverb, or I for interjection.

_____ 7. Great! We can leave now.

_____ 8. You taste with your tongue, your nose, and your brain.

_____ 9. Brandi is an excellent soccer player; likewise, she is a talented gymnast.

_____ 10. A male walrus may weigh 3,000 pounds, yet a female rarely exceeds 2,000 pounds.

_____ 11. Well! I can't believe it!

_____ 12. It's not healthy to eat a lot of sugar; nevertheless, it's okay to treat yourself sometimes.

_____ 13. The actress wore an old but beautiful dress.

# CHAPTER 18  Prepositions, Conjunctions, and Interjections Review

**EXERCISE** Identify the underlined word or words by writing P for preposition, C for conjunction, CA for conjunctive adverb, or I for interjection.

_____ 1. Pastries and fruit were offered <u>at</u> the breakfast buffet.

_____ 2. <u>Both</u> Katie <u>and</u> Scott said they can volunteer at the fund-raiser.

_____ 3. I had to write a paper last night; <u>otherwise</u>, I could have gone to the game.

_____ 4. A hot-air balloon drifted <u>above</u> our heads.

_____ 5. <u>Hooray</u>! You got an A on your math test!

_____ 6. Tim's band will play <u>at</u> my birthday party.

_____ 7. I've never gone skiing before; <u>nevertheless</u>, I'd like to give it a try.

_____ 8. We were all full, <u>yet</u> no one could resist the homemade chocolate cake.

_____ 9. <u>Ouch</u>! I just stubbed my toe!

_____ 10. I'd be happy to walk your dog; <u>besides</u>, I need some exercise anyhow.

_____ 11. <u>On</u> long car rides, my legs get stiff.

_____ 12. After their walk, the dogs were tired <u>but</u> happy.

_____ 13. Melvin found his pet snake <u>under</u> the bed.

_____ 14. Some bananas are picked green <u>and</u> fried in batter.

_____ 15. <u>Wow</u>! That was a lucky shot.

_____ 16. <u>Neither</u> ostriches <u>nor</u> penguins can fly.

_____ 17. Red foxes live around the world; <u>however</u>, they are seldom seen.

_____ 18. Wild turkeys were hunted <u>by</u> American pioneers.

## CHAPTER 18 — Other Parts of Speech Review

**EXERCISE** Identify the part of speech of the underlined word or words in each sentence.

_____ 1. Stale bread sometimes gets moldy.
   A adjective
   B adverb
   C noun
   D pronoun

_____ 2. A friend from school played me his new CDs.
   A reflexive pronoun
   B personal pronoun
   C intensive pronoun
   D indefinite pronoun

_____ 3. The tomb of Johnny Appleseed is in Fort Wayne, Indiana.
   A adjective
   B preposition
   C pronoun
   D noun

_____ 4. What is your answer to this question?
   A noun
   B pronoun
   C adjective
   D adverb

_____ 5. During the summer, fresh corn is available.
   A transitive verb
   B helping verb
   C linking verb
   D intransitive verb

_____ 6. The baby can now walk and talk.
   A verb
   B adjective
   C adverb
   D pronoun

_____ 7. Those kittens are adorable!
   A adjective
   B pronoun
   C preposition
   D pronoun

_____ 8. I swam across the pool quickly.
   A linking verb
   B helping verb
   C transitive verb
   D intransitive verb

_____ 9. They canoed down the Saint Clair River.
   A proper noun
   B compound noun
   C personal pronoun
   D indefinite pronoun

_____ 10. In May 1933, six boys suddenly became national heroes.
   A adjective
   B adverb
   C preposition
   D verb

_____ 11. At dusk, we were walking quietly along the railroad tracks.
   A noun
   B adverb
   C verb
   D adjective

_____ 12. All of them lived in a home for orphans.
   A pronoun
   B preposition
   C adjective
   D adverb

Name _____    Date _____

# CHAPTER 19   Direct Objects

**[19B]** A **direct object** is a noun or pronoun that answers the question *What?* or *Whom?* after an action verb.

**EXERCISE A** Select the direct object in each sentence.

_____ 1. Butterflies have hollow tongues.
    **A** hollow
    **B** tongues
    **C** Butterflies

_____ 2. William Tell pierced the apple on his son's head with an arrow.
    **A** arrow
    **B** head
    **C** apple

_____ 3. Camels provide leather for millions of people.
    **A** leather
    **B** millions
    **C** people

_____ 4. Martha plays the flute very well.
    **A** well
    **B** flute
    **C** Martha

_____ 5. Early settlers used whale oil in their lamps.
    **A** oil
    **B** settlers
    **C** lamps

_____ 6. The plane delivered our packages.
    **A** plane
    **B** packages
    **C** delivered

**EXERCISE B** Underline the direct object in each of the following sentences.

7. We placed a CD in the time capsule.

8. The Greeks used mirrors of brass and bronze.

9. Everyone enjoyed the clowns at the circus.

10. For breakfast, I had cereal.

11. Mom planted a birch tree in our front yard.

12. Have you ever owned any goldfish?

13. I have a math test tomorrow.

14. My brother knows them very well.

Name _____ Date _____

# CHAPTER 19  Indirect Objects

**[19B]** An **indirect object** is a noun or pronoun that answers the question *To or for whom?* or *To or for what?* after an action verb.

> **EXERCISE** Write the word that is the indirect object in each sentence.

_____  1. The captain gave his teammates a pep talk.

_____  2. The Native American sold the settlers corn.

_____  3. Yasuko gave me a cricket for a pet.

_____  4. Mexico sells our country oil and gas.

_____  5. The coach offered Frank some good advice.

_____  6. The elephant gave its baby a bath.

_____  7. Did you pick her a bunch of wildflowers?

_____  8. Please show everyone this poster.

_____  9. Betsy made Tony a map of her neighborhood.

_____  10. Our neighbors loaned us their new tent.

_____  11. Mrs. Roberts paid Harry his salary.

_____  12. Billy offered Beth a ride to town.

_____  13. Did he give Karen a pair of skates?

_____  14. Giselle wrote me a letter.

_____  15. Before bed, Mary told her brother a scary story.

# CHAPTER 19  Direct and Indirect Objects

**EXERCISE** Underline the direct object once and the indirect object twice in each of the following sentences.

1. I baked them strawberry and vanilla cupcakes.

2. After the race, the winner gave herself a pat on the back.

3. Matthew sent Natalie his new address and phone number.

4. Aiden drew Logan a map of their bike route.

5. Ethel handed Hannah the luggage from the backseat.

6. The coach offered Luke some gentle advice.

7. Mark made me a birthday present.

8. Samson sold Lorenzo his football tickets.

9. Hunter built the children a huge tree house.

10. Please pass Jocelyn the mashed potatoes.

11. You should show the class your new painting.

12. Marco bought Rihanna a gold necklace.

# CHAPTER 19 Predicate Nominatives

**[19C]** A **predicate nominative** is a noun or a pronoun that follows a linking verb and identifies, renames, or explains the subject.

> **EXERCISE** Underline the predicate nominative in each sentence.

1. A seahorse is a fish with a long snout.
2. September is the ninth month of our year.
3. Christopher Columbus was probably an Italian by birth.
4. The roller coaster has become the favorite ride at the amusement park.
5. The Rio Grande is the border between Texas and Mexico.
6. That bright object must be the North Star.
7. The new restaurant on this block will be a cafeteria.
8. Vegetables are essential foods.
9. Amelia Earhart became a famous pilot.
10. A turtle's shell may be leathery skin.
11. Ted will remain captain of the team next year.
12. The director of the bank last year was Mrs. Snow.
13. Someday I may be a politician.
14. The animal in that pen is a walrus.
15. One of my favorite subjects is math.
16. Dr. Fredericks is my dentist.
17. The name of my hometown is Trinity.

Name _____   Date _____

# CHAPTER 19  Predicate Adjectives

**[19C]** A **predicate adjective** is an adjective that follows a linking verb and modifies the subject.

**EXERCISE A** Select the answer that shows all the predicate adjectives in each sentence below.

_____ 1. A snake's skin is dry and smooth.
- A  skin, dry
- B  dry, smooth
- C  snake's, smooth

_____ 2. Pine trees are always green.
- A  green
- B  trees, green
- C  Pine, green

_____ 3. The throat of this male hummingbird is red.
- A  throat, red
- B  male, red
- C  red

_____ 4. The roasting turkey smells really delicious.
- A  roasting, delicious
- B  delicious
- C  really, delicious

_____ 5. The forest looked dense and green.
- A  forest, green
- B  dense, forest
- C  dense, green

_____ 6. Potatoes can be white or yellow.
- A  white
- B  yellow
- C  white, yellow

**EXERCISE B** Write the predicate adjective or compound predicate adjective in each of following sentences.

_____ 7. At the end of the day, the hikers were still happy and peppy.

_____ 8. Whales are very intelligent.

_____ 9. The grass grew tall and thick.

_____ 10. Pure gold is soft.

_____ 11. The flowers in the bouquet were red and purple.

_____ 12. The rolls were warm and buttery.

_____ 13. After the race, Mariah felt very tired.

_____ 14. Before the storm, the horses all seemed nervous.

# CHAPTER 19 Complements Review

**EXERCISE** Identify the term that correctly describes the underlined word or words.

_____ 1. Sam gave me a <u>ride</u> to the store.
   A  direct object
   B  indirect object
   C  predicate nominative
   D  predicate adjective

_____ 2. The trainer tossed the <u>seal</u> a fresh fish.
   A  direct object
   B  indirect object
   C  predicate nominative
   D  predicate adjective

_____ 3. Tammy was <u>one</u> of the riders.
   A  direct object
   B  indirect object
   C  predicate nominative
   D  predicate adjective

_____ 4. Nat sent <u>Rosa</u> a picture postcard from Dallas.
   A  direct object
   B  indirect object
   C  predicate nominative
   D  predicate adjective

_____ 5. Did you tell me your <u>address</u>?
   A  direct object
   B  indirect object
   C  predicate nominative
   D  predicate adjective

_____ 6. These vegetables are nearly <u>ripe</u>.
   A  direct object
   B  indirect object
   C  predicate nominative
   D  predicate adjective

_____ 7. The pilot told the <u>audience</u> his adventure.
   A  direct object
   B  indirect object
   C  predicate nominative
   D  predicate adjective

_____ 8. Human tears are <u>salty</u>.
   A  direct object
   B  indirect object
   C  predicate nominative
   D  predicate adjective

_____ 9. Please pass <u>him</u> the salad.
   A  direct object
   B  indirect object
   C  predicate nominative
   D  predicate adjective

_____ 10. Spring has become my favorite <u>season</u>.
   A  direct object
   B  indirect object
   C  predicate nominative
   D  predicate adjective

_____ 11. A guidance counselor must be a good <u>listener</u>.
   A  direct object
   B  indirect object
   C  predicate nominative
   D  predicate adjective

_____ 12. Arianna collects <u>stamps</u> for a hobby.
   A  direct object
   B  indirect object
   C  predicate nominative
   D  predicate adjective

Name _____  Date _____

# CHAPTER 20  Prepositional Phrases

**[20A]** A **prepositional phrase** is a group of words that begins with a preposition, ends with a noun or a pronoun, and is used as an adjective or adverb.

---

**EXERCISE A** Select the prepositional phrase in each sentence.

---

_____ 1. The automobiles with power steering are the only ones I can drive.
   A  I can drive
   B  with power steering
   C  are the only ones I can drive

_____ 2. The sweater on the table is the ugliest sweater I have seen.
   A  I have seen
   B  the ugliest sweater
   C  on the table

_____ 3. The shade tree near the campus is Melissa and Susan's favorite.
   A  near the campus
   B  Melissa and Susan's favorite
   C  The shade tree near the campus

_____ 4. You are exactly the kind of person we want.
   A  the kind of person
   B  of person
   C  exactly the kind

_____ 5. The criminal was last seen running toward the post office.
   A  running toward the post office
   B  was last seen
   C  toward the post office

_____ 6. Samson is the culprit who threw the watermelon down the stairs.
   A  the watermelon down the stairs
   B  the culprit who threw
   C  down the stairs

---

**EXERCISE B** Underline the prepositional phrase in each sentence.

---

7. Last weekend, I wrote a report about the Boston Tea Party.

8. A very honest and friendly person, Mrs. Williams often makes cookies for her grateful neighbors.

9. The green and gold snake began moving briskly toward the cellar door.

10. By approximately three o'clock, I will already be sleeping soundly.

11. Those boots make you look like a jockey.

12. The soccer ball soared over the players' heads.

13. The snow throughout April and May was quite a surprise this year.

Name _____  Date _____

# CHAPTER 20  Adjectival Phrases

**[20A.1]** An **adjectival phrase** is a prepositional phrase that modifies a noun or pronoun.

**EXERCISE A** Select the word that is modified by the underlined adjectival phrase in each sentence.

_____ 1. The highest point <u>on Earth</u> is Mount Everest.
   A  Mount Everest
   B  point
   C  highest

_____ 2. The sky <u>over Mount Washington</u> was completely cloudless.
   A  sky
   B  cloudless
   C  completely

_____ 3. That diver found the box <u>with the gold coins</u>.
   A  diver
   B  found
   C  box

_____ 4. The house <u>across the lake</u> is 100 years old.
   A  years
   B  old
   C  house

_____ 5. Did you see the road <u>near the old bridge</u>?
   A  you
   B  road
   C  see

_____ 6. Comets are mysterious wanderers <u>in space</u>.
   A  Comets
   B  wanderers
   C  mysterious

**EXERCISE B** Write the word that is modified by the underlined adjectival phrase in each sentence.

_____ 7. Communication is an exchange <u>of information</u>.

_____ 8. People <u>in communities</u> share many customs.

_____ 9. The postcard <u>from Hilda</u> is on the table.

_____ 10. The Big Dipper is a familiar group <u>of stars</u>.

_____ 11. The stars <u>in the sky</u> look close together.

_____ 12. Every country <u>in the world</u> has its own folk tales.

_____ 13. Here is a good view <u>of Chicago</u>.

# CHAPTER 20  Adjectival Phrases

**EXERCISE** Underline the adjectival phrase in each sentence. Then circle the word the adjectival phrase modifies.

1. The (coal) in this area was once peat.

2. I read an (article) about the ocean floor.

3. I bought the (shoes) on that shelf.

4. The (table) against the wall is an antique.

5. A (network) of roads connected Incan cities.

6. A (hedge) with sharp thorns lined the front sidewalk.

7. The (lamp) on the desk never works.

8. James liked the (story) about wild horses.

9. (One) of my friends wrote an essay.

10. The (package) by the door is a gift.

11. The most dangerous (animal) in the Far North is the polar bear.

12. The first (batter) on the home team hit a home run.

13. The Camerons own the (apartment) below us.

14. The apatosaurus was a tremendous (dinosaur) with a long tail and a small head.

# CHAPTER 20  Misplaced Adjectival Phrases

**[20A.2]** When an adjectival phrase is placed too far from the word it describes, it is called a **misplaced modifier**. A misplaced modifier can confuse readers.

> **EXERCISE** Rewrite each sentence so that the adjectival phrase is in the correct position.

1. The police officer gave tickets without licenses to the drivers.

2. The driver has an excellent driving record in the red car.

3. That riding stable is closed across the road.

4. The biggest book is *War and Peace* in our library.

5. The child was playing from the next street.

6. The horse was running with the black spots on his shoulder.

7. My mother gave coupons to the children for free ice cream.

8. The cottage is vacant across the lake.

9. The path was narrow through the pine woods.

10. Six students organized the pancake breakfast on the committee.

11. The sailboat left the race with a torn sail.

# CHAPTER 20  Adverbial Phrases

**[20A.3]** An **adverbial phrase** is a prepositional phrase that is used mainly to modify a verb.

**EXERCISE** Circle the word or words each underlined adverbial phrase modifies.

1. Rice is grown <u>in Chinese valleys</u>.

2. Many early cities were built <u>around forts</u>.

3. Clay is mined <u>for industry</u>.

4. <u>During the winter</u>, many people skate.

5. <u>In the Middle Ages</u>, every royal court had a clown.

6. <u>Over the years</u>, dress styles change.

7. Steel can be formed <u>into any shape</u>.

8. The satellite moved <u>across the sky</u>.

9. <u>Before dawn</u>, the birds sang loudly.

10. <u>In spring</u>, many rivers flood their banks.

11. Nearly all fish are covered <u>with scales</u>.

12. Early explorers sailed <u>without compasses</u>.

13. Weather satellites circle <u>above the earth</u>.

14. <u>In colonial days</u>, no fire departments existed.

15. Frost forms <u>on cold winter mornings</u>.

# CHAPTER 20 Adverbial Phrases

**EXERCISE** In the chart below, write each adverbial phrase and the word or words it modifies.

1. Paul Revere's house is on this street.

2. During the American Revolution, people flew many different flags.

3. Water rolled off the seal's skin.

4. Behind the wall, we found a secret garden.

5. The Blue Ridge Parkway runs along mountain ridges.

6. Before intermission, my sister left the play.

7. In art class, I must finish my clay pot.

8. I have gone to the city library on several occasions.

9. Within an hour, we will know the winners.

10. A narrow road wound around the steep cliff.

| | Adverbial Phrase | Word(s) It Modifies |
|---|---|---|
| 1. | | |
| 2. | | |
| 3. | | |
| 4. | | |
| 5. | | |
| 6. | | |
| 7. | | |
| 8. | | |
| 9. | | |
| 10. | | |

Name _____ Date _____

# CHAPTER 20  Appositives and Appositive Phrases

**[20B]** An **appositive** is a noun or pronoun that identifies or explains another noun or pronoun in the sentence. When an appositive has a modifier, it is called an **appositive phrase**.

> **EXERCISE** Write the appositive or appositive phrase in each sentence.

1. Stephanie, the student council president, wants to volunteer at the food bank.
   _____

2. The movie *Star Wars* is a science fiction classic.
   _____

3. Mrs. Guerrero, our social studies teacher, is retiring.
   _____

4. My brother will play on the neighborhood team, the Mustangs.
   _____

5. The fireman, the one with the badge, talked to the students about fire safety.
   _____

6. The song "We Are the Champions" was played after we won the championship.
   _____

7. Mr. Peretti taught us about the First Amendment, the Free Speech Amendment.
   _____

8. Our cat, the one with the blue collar, is always getting into trouble.
   _____

9. Justin, my brother, was responsible for planning the birthday party.
   _____

10. My favorite teacher, Mrs. Smith, assigns us many interesting books to read.
    _____

11. *WALL-E*, an animated movie about a robot, won an Oscar®.
    _____

12. The book *The Call of the Wild* is one of my favorites.
    _____

# CHAPTER 20  Phrases Review

**EXERCISE** Write the letter of the term that correctly identifies the underlined word or words in the paragraph below.

Many fishermen collect worms **(1)** <u>at night</u>. Worms, **(2)** <u>the favorite meal of fish</u>, are used as bait. Manuel Romero, **(3)** <u>a fisherman in Florida</u>, catches worms **(4)** <u>in a special way</u>. First, he pokes a stick **(5)** <u>with a pointed end</u> **(6)** <u>into</u> the earth. Then he rubs a piece **(7)** <u>of steel</u> **(8)** <u>across</u> the top of the stick, causing the ground around the stick to vibrate. This action, **(9)** <u>a kind of beckoning</u>, brings worms **(10)** <u>to the surface</u>. **(11)** <u>On a good day</u>, he may harvest two hundred worms. He sells his extra supply to other fishermen **(12)** <u>in the area</u>.

_____ 1. **A** adjectival phrase
     **B** adverbial phrase
     **C** appositive phrase
     **D** preposition

_____ 2. **A** adjectival phrase
     **B** adverbial phrase
     **C** appositive phrase
     **D** preposition

_____ 3. **A** adjectival phrase
     **B** adverbial phrase
     **C** appositive phrase
     **D** preposition

_____ 4. **A** adjectival phrase
     **B** adverbial phrase
     **C** appositive phrase
     **D** preposition

_____ 5. **A** adjectival phrase
     **B** adverbial phrase
     **C** appositive phrase
     **D** preposition

_____ 6. **A** adjectival phrase
     **B** adverbial phrase
     **C** appositive phrase
     **D** preposition

_____ 7. **A** adjectival phrase
     **B** adverbial phrase
     **C** appositive phrase
     **D** preposition

_____ 8. **A** adjectival phrase
     **B** adverbial phrase
     **C** appositive phrase
     **D** preposition

_____ 9. **A** adjectival phrase
     **B** adverbial phrase
     **C** appositive phrase
     **D** preposition

_____ 10. **A** adjectival phrase
     **B** adverbial phrase
     **C** appositive phrase
     **D** preposition

_____ 11. **A** adjectival phrase
     **B** adverbial phrase
     **C** appositive phrase
     **D** preposition

_____ 12. **A** adjectival phrase
     **B** adverbial phrase
     **C** appositive phrase
     **D** preposition

# CHAPTER 21  Participles

**[21A.1]** A **participle** is a verb form that is used as an adjective.

**EXERCISE A**  Choose the participle in each sentence.

_____ 1. The moving van was parked beneath the tree.
   A  moving
   B  parked
   C  beneath

_____ 2. The beaten eggs are in the bowl.
   A  eggs
   B  bowl
   C  beaten

_____ 3. I enjoy freezing temperatures in winter.
   A  enjoy
   B  freezing
   C  winter

_____ 4. The growling dog scared the children away.
   A  scared
   B  growling
   C  children

_____ 5. The whistling wind made an eerie sound at night.
   A  made
   B  eerie
   C  whistling

_____ 6. We ate frozen yogurt Saturday night.
   A  frozen
   B  yogurt
   C  night

**EXERCISE B**  Underline the participle in each sentence. Then circle the word it modifies.

7. Singing birds can brighten any day.

8. Have you seen the lost mittens?

9. We took the beaten path into the forest.

10. The ticking clock could be heard throughout the house.

11. The falling snow was white and cold.

12. My sister took riding lessons at a stable.

13. The frosted windows were too cold to touch.

14. The skating party will be held on Friday.

Name _____   Date _____

## CHAPTER 21  Parciple or Verb?

**EXERCISE** Write P if the underlined word is a participle or V if it is a verb.

_____ 1. The <u>washing</u> machine was making a horrible sound.

_____ 2. We had <u>taken</u> the train to Michigan.

_____ 3. The <u>singing</u> children were quite entertaining.

_____ 4. Our apartment building is <u>locked</u> at night.

_____ 5. My brother is <u>looking</u> for a new car.

_____ 6. The <u>cracked</u> teapot could not be fixed.

_____ 7. My grandmother has many <u>baking</u> supplies.

_____ 8. I would like to take a <u>cooking</u> class.

_____ 9. Are you <u>sewing</u> your costume for the party?

_____ 10. Charlie's <u>sewing</u> machine is in the closet.

_____ 11. We will be <u>fishing</u> this weekend.

_____ 12. I used <u>cleaning</u> fluid on my silver ring.

_____ 13. My sister is <u>cleaning</u> her room this afternoon.

_____ 14. Our teacher is <u>making</u> cookies for our party.

_____ 15. We spilled crumbs on the <u>swept</u> floor.

_____ 16. Dakota is <u>listening</u> to her favorite CD.

Name _____ Date _____

### CHAPTER 21 — Participial Phrases

**[21A.2]** A **participial phrase** is a participle joined with related words. The related words in a participial phrase often include a complement, an adverb, or an adverbial phrase.

> **EXERCISE** Underline the participial phrase in each of the following sentences.

1. Driving through the snow, my father had to use caution.
2. The dinner, cooking on the stove, smelled wonderful.
3. Pushing the wagon up the hill, the paperboy continued to deliver papers.
4. Riding my bicycle, I began to breathe heavily.
5. Listening carefully, I heard the instructions from the teacher.
6. Racing to the finish line, I smiled victoriously.
7. Showering the fields, the rain fell all day.
8. Eating the spicy food, I began to sweat.
9. My band, marching in the contest, took the audience by surprise.
10. My aunt, living along the coast, is used to hurricane winds.
11. Joel, smiling after the win, joined his teammates on the field.
12. The actor, overtaken by fans, hurried into the hotel.
13. My sister, wearing her prom dress, looked beautiful.
14. Rochelle, studying all evening, missed the game.

Name _____   Date _____

## CHAPTER 21 — Misplaced Participial Phrases

**EXERCISE** Rewrite each sentence so that the participial phrase is in the proper place.

1. Tad saw the ice cream truck riding his bike.

2. Playing the guitar, the cat was fascinated with John.

3. Britney heard a band reading in the park.

4. George noticed a small bird sitting quietly on a bench.

5. Jackson and Dylan watched a duck waiting for their sodas.

6. The principal noticed some trash walking through the halls.

7. The children saw a tiger standing in line for the water fountain.

8. Jeremy bumped into my mother turning suddenly.

9. Melia passed the mall crossing the bridge.

10. Ruby showed us the scar holding her dog.

Name _____  Date _____

# CHAPTER 21  Infinitives

**[21A.3]** An **infinitive** is a verb form that usually beings with *to*. It is used as a noun, an adjective, or an adverb.

**EXERCISE A** Write the infinitive in each sentence.

_____ 1. We wanted to dance.

_____ 2. Sara tried to sing.

_____ 3. When you get older, you will need to work.

_____ 4. To fly is my goal.

_____ 5. The coach expects to win.

_____ 6. Maria went to study.

_____ 7. Are you sure this is the trail to follow?

_____ 8. Sam said he wanted to eat.

**EXERCISE B** Underline the infinitive in each sentence. Then identify whether the infinitive is used as a noun, an adjective, or an adverb by writing *noun*, *adjective*, or *adverb* on the blank.

_____ 9. To sleep is difficult with all this noise.

_____ 10. Malia wants to win.

_____ 11. My favorite shirt to wear is dirty.

_____ 12. They met at the track to run.

_____ 13. To finish will take forever.

_____ 14. Which is the best dessert to order?

_____ 15. We must practice to improve.

_____ 16. Those are the buttons to use.

# CHAPTER 21  Infinitive or Prepositional Phrase?

**EXERCISE** Write I if the underlined phrase is an infinitive or P if it is a prepositional phrase.

_____ 1. We went <u>to the mall</u> yesterday.

_____ 2. My father is driving a truck <u>to make</u> a living.

_____ 3. They drove <u>to work</u> this morning.

_____ 4. We are going <u>to town</u> tonight.

_____ 5. He gave the DVD <u>to her</u>.

_____ 6. We took my dog <u>to the vet</u>.

_____ 7. We wanted <u>to play</u> ball with the team.

_____ 8. We drove <u>to the play</u> last night.

_____ 9. Driving <u>to town</u>, my father was cautious.

_____ 10. I want <u>to plan</u> the party after school.

_____ 11. Everything went according <u>to plan</u>.

_____ 12. We went <u>to eat</u> at the restaurant.

_____ 13. We can research and contribute <u>to science</u>.

_____ 14. I took the bus <u>to school</u>.

_____ 15. I want <u>to school</u> myself in astronomy.

_____ 16. I can learn anything if I go <u>to class</u>.

_____ 17. He went <u>to speak</u> at the assembly.

# CHAPTER 21  Infinitive Phrases

**[21A.4]** An **infinitive phrase** is an infinitive with its modifiers and complements—all working together as a noun, adjective, or adverb.

**EXERCISE A** Select the infinitive phrase for each sentence.

_____ 1. We went to run last Saturday night.
    A  We went to run
    B  to run
    C  to run last Saturday night

_____ 2. My brother learned to play well.
    A  learned to
    B  My brother
    C  to play well

_____ 3. I want to go to the movies tomorrow.
    A  to go to the movies tomorrow
    B  I want to go
    C  to the movies tomorrow

_____ 4. Our dog likes to sit on the couch.
    A  to sit on the couch
    B  Our dog
    C  likes to sit

_____ 5. Our cat likes to sit with him.
    A  Our cat
    B  likes to sit
    C  to sit with him

_____ 6. We went to eat at a restaurant in town.
    A  to eat at a restaurant in town
    B  at a restaurant in town
    C  We went to eat

**EXERCISE B** Underline the infinitive phrase in each of the following sentences.

7. I like to play music on my stereo.

8. To ease our anxiety, we reviewed for the test.

9. Training wheels help a child to ride a bike.

10. To work on a paper, you need a good dictionary.

11. While studying, you need to sit in a quiet room.

12. To ride well, you should take lessons.

13. To play football, you need passing grades.

# CHAPTER 21 Verbals and Verbal Phrases Review

**EXERCISE** Write the letter of the term that correctly describes the underlined word or words.

_____ 1. The <u>broken</u> glass lay in pieces on the floor.
  A infinitive
  B verb
  C participle
  D infinitive phrase

_____ 2. Jorge passed the comic book store <u>crossing the highway</u>.
  A misplaced participial phrase
  B infinitive phrase
  C prepositional phrase
  D verb

_____ 3. Rebecca likes <u>to watch movies on her computer</u>.
  A participial phrase
  B infinitive phrase
  C prepositional phrase
  D infinitive

_____ 4. <u>Running to catch the bus</u>, Nora yelled, "Wait for me!"
  A prepositional phrase
  B participle
  C infinitive phrase
  D participial phrase

_____ 5. Maddox was asked <u>to speak</u> at the meeting last night.
  A infinitive
  B misplaced participial phrase
  C prepositional phrase
  D infinitive phrase

_____ 6. We were <u>playing</u> chess at Avery's house.
  A participle
  B infinitive
  C verb
  D preposition

_____ 7. I took the number 15 bus <u>to the library</u>.
  A infinitive phrase
  B participle
  C participial phrase
  D prepositional phrase

_____ 8. Henry wants <u>to research</u> the history of his state.
  A infinitive
  B participial phrase
  C prepositional phrase
  D infinitive phrase

_____ 9. <u>Pushing the sled up the hill</u>, the kids continued to enjoy the snow.
  A prepositional phrase
  B infinitive phrase
  C participial phrase
  D participle

_____ 10. <u>To draw well</u>, you should practice drawing daily.
  A misplaced participial phrase
  B infinitive phrase
  C prepositional phrase
  D infinitive

_____ 11. The <u>crashing</u> box made a loud noise on the sidewalk.
  A preposition
  B verb
  C infinitive
  D participle

_____ 12. Sonia found some missing birthday cards <u>sorting through her desk</u>.
  A infinitive phrase
  B prepositional phrase
  C misplaced participial phrase
  D verb

Name _____ Date _____

# CHAPTER 22  Independent and Subordinate Clauses

**[22A.1]** An **independent, or main, clause** can stand alone as a sentence because it expresses a complete idea.

**[22A.2]** A **subordinate, or dependent, clause** cannot stand alone as sentence because it does not express a complete thought.

> **EXERCISE A** Write I if the underlined clause is an independent clause or S if it is a subordinate clause.

_____ 1. <u>Because I cannot swim</u>, I seldom go to the beach.

_____ 2. <u>Anne cleared the table</u> before Lou washed the dishes.

_____ 3. I have the correct time <u>unless my watch stopped</u>.

_____ 4. <u>While you go inside</u>, Kay will wait over there.

_____ 5. Unless I finish this paper, <u>I can't go to the party</u>.

_____ 6. I like these jeans <u>because they fit so well</u>.

_____ 7. Since it's so hot, <u>let's turn on the air conditioning</u>.

_____ 8. <u>We will celebrate</u> when Liz gets home.

> **EXERCISE B** Underline each independent clause once and each subordinate clause twice in the sentences below.

9. Before the movie started, we made some popcorn.

10. Although we already have two cats, we kept the kitten.

11. I played basketball after I cleaned my room.

12. The mail carrier rang the doorbell as I was taking the cake out of the oven.

13. If you're feeling under the weather, you should stay home and rest.

14. You use many muscles as you say just one word.

15. When you sleep, you dream about twenty percent of the time.

16. Even though it was late, I couldn't fall asleep.

17. Antonio reached second base because the shortstop's throw was wild.

# CHAPTER 22  Adverbial Clauses

**[22B.1]** An **adverbial clause** is a subordinate clause that is used mainly to modify a verb.

> **EXERCISE** Underline the adverbial clause in each sentence. Then circle the verb or verb phrase that the clause modifies.

1. Mom and Dad (left) <u>after the storm had ended</u>.

2. Beth (looked) <u>as if she had seen a ghost</u>.

3. <u>When Susan speaks</u>, people (listen).

4. Wolves (hunt) <u>where they can find plenty of game</u>.

5. Valerie (memorized) her lines <u>until she knew them by heart</u>.

6. You (should bring) your swimsuit <u>so that you can swim</u>.

7. <u>When the campers return from the hike</u>, they (will be) thirsty.

8. <u>Because Gordon's mother speaks French</u>, he (passes) French class.

9. <u>Until Chuck was ten</u>, he (hated) vegetables.

10. <u>When we landed at the airport</u>, it (was raining).

11. <u>Before we could travel abroad</u>, we (had to get) our passports.

12. We (had) plenty of food <u>because Dad cooked all week</u>.

# CHAPTER 22  Subordinating Conjunctions

**EXERCISE** Write the subordinating conjunction(s) in each sentence.

_____ 1. After the storm was over, a rainbow appeared.

_____ 2. Unless you plan to go skiing, you won't need much money.

_____ 3. I have been playing the flute since I was five.

_____ 4. Lola danced as though she didn't know the judges were there.

_____ 5. I will work until I have enough money for a new laptop computer.

_____ 6. Although the sky was cloudy, Arthur left for the beach.

_____ 7. Jill stood on tiptoe so she could see the performance.

_____ 8. Because I forgot my camera, I didn't have any pictures of my trip.

_____ 9. When you read a lot of books, you learn a lot.

_____ 10. Mom opened the windows so that we could feel the spring breeze.

_____ 11. Before you go outside, put on a hat.

_____ 12. As far as I could see, birds filled the bay.

_____ 13. Jody stayed up late even though she had a test in the morning.

_____ 14. My uncle comes to visit us whenever he can.

_____ 15. As the students grew more confident, their performance improved.

_____ 16. That dog looks as if he is smiling.

_____ 17. Put your things where you like.

_____ 18. As long as no one bothers him, the cat will be fine.

_____ 19. Wherever you go, remember your manners!

_____ 20. Though it was a long trip, Lance enjoyed the train ride.

Name _____ Date _____

# CHAPTER 22  Adjectival Clauses

**[22B.2]** An **adjectival clause** is a subordinate clause that is used to modify a noun or pronoun.

> **EXERCISE** Underline the adjectival clause in each sentence. Then write the noun or pronoun that the clause modifies.

_____ 1. This is not the sweater that I had in mind.

_____ 2. We enjoyed the peaches that we picked this afternoon.

_____ 3. Did you tell her about the time that you fell at the skating rink?

_____ 4. This is my sister Melanie, whom I was telling you about.

_____ 5. The book that you loaned me was good.

_____ 6. Ashley, who had just returned from vacation, was tired.

_____ 7. It was Levi Strauss who invented blue jeans.

_____ 8. This is the kitten that I want.

_____ 9. I know the park that you are talking about.

_____ 10. Mr. Conroy was the one who asked about you.

_____ 11. The car, which had a flat tire, was parked on the side of the road.

_____ 12. The band that is the best costs too much money.

_____ 13. Aunt Myrna is the one who called us.

# CHAPTER 22  Misplaced Adjectival Clauses

**EXERCISE** Rewrite each sentence so that the adjectival clause is in the correct place.

1. Shelly took the apples and made a pie that we picked this afternoon.
   _____

2. Sean saw a rabbit who was very quiet.
   _____

3. People waited in line who wanted to see the movie.
   _____

4. The boy picked up the bag who wore a red sweater.
   _____

5. The party was quiet which was held last night.
   _____

6. Donnie caught a wave who enjoys surfing.
   _____

7. Perry tasted the cake who never really likes chocolate.
   _____

8. A gull begged for a potato chip that was flying just above us.
   _____

9. Ken explored the seashore whose love for the beach is great.
   _____

10. Some kids played in the water who had a raft.
    _____

11. The children rushed into the waves who were eager to swim.
    _____

# CHAPTER 22  Simple and Compound Sentences

**[22C.1]** A **simple sentence** is a sentence that has one subject and one verb.
**[22C.2]** A **compound sentence** is made up of two or more simple sentences, usually joined by a comma and a coordinating conjunction: *and, but, or,* or *yet.*

> **EXERCISE** Write S if the sentence is a simple sentence or C if it a compound sentence.

_____ 1. Amelia Earhart was a pioneer in the field of flying.

_____ 2. The picnic will begin at noon, but the buses will leave at nine o'clock.

_____ 3. In ancient China children played with kites, but boats were favorite toys in ancient Rome.

_____ 4. Carrie is working at the computer.

_____ 5. I cleaned the fish, and my brother cooked them over the campfire.

_____ 6. Tumbleweeds blow off across open spaces.

_____ 7. Each rolling tumbleweed drops new seeds, and many new plants take hold.

_____ 8. Clouds are formed from water particles in the air.

_____ 9. Peanuts are a good source of protein.

_____ 10. On advice from the Native Americans, the Pilgrims planted corn.

_____ 11. Sharon gave me this sweater, but it doesn't fit.

_____ 12. After the meeting, Joe turned off all the lights.

_____ 13. Insects have six legs, but spiders have eight legs.

_____ 14. I waited for two hours, but nobody came.

_____ 15. The sun is shining, but rain is predicted.

_____ 16. Jennifer is flying her new kite in the park.

_____ 17. I will join the school band next year.

_____ 18. Bill's parakeet is green, but mine is blue.

# CHAPTER 22 Compound Sentence or Compound Verb?

**EXERCISE** Choose whether the sentence has a compound verb or whether it is a compound sentence.

_____ 1. I made the beds, and Colleen ran the vacuum.
   A compound verb
   B compound sentence

_____ 2. The plastic bags flew from my hand and blew across the parking lot.
   A compound verb
   B compound sentence

_____ 3. Amelia Earhart flew alone across the Atlantic and made the first solo flight from California to Hawaii.
   A compound verb
   B compound sentence

_____ 4. Martin is reading in the shade or is playing with his brother.
   A compound verb
   B compound sentence

_____ 5. At the party, Judy was dressed as a clown, but Carlos came as Abraham Lincoln.
   A compound verb
   B compound sentence

_____ 6. The moon rose over the mountain and flooded the campsite with moonlight.
   A compound verb
   B compound sentence

_____ 7. Thunder roared, and lightning flashed across the sky.
   A compound verb
   B compound sentence

_____ 8. The baby owl blinked and trembled in the bright light.
   A compound verb
   B compound sentence

_____ 9. The train pulled into the station, and many commuters got off.
   A compound verb
   B compound sentence

_____ 10. You prepare the salad, and I will cook the stew.
   A compound verb
   B compound sentence

_____ 11. The storm broke suddenly and grew still.
   A compound verb
   B compound sentence

_____ 12. Chickens have wishbones, but parrots do not.
   A compound verb
   B compound sentence

_____ 13. I will water the garden, and Jill will cut the grass.
   A compound verb
   B compound sentence

_____ 14. Sara will buy the cake and decorate it.
   A compound verb
   B compound sentence

_____ 15. Some animals hibernate during the winter and sleep under heavy snow.
   A compound verb
   B compound sentence

Name _____  Date _____

# CHAPTER 22  Complex Sentences

**[22C.3]** A **complex sentence** consists of one independent clause and one or more subordinate clauses.

**EXERCISE A**  Write *YES* if the sentence is a complex sentence. Write *NO* if it is not a complex sentence.

_____ 1. After you have seen the school nurse, please report back to the classroom.

_____ 2. Our kitten ran down the hallway and into my bedroom.

_____ 3. Norman Rockwell illustrated many covers of the *Saturday Evening Post*, which my grandparents used to read often.

_____ 4. When I read Longfellow's poem, I wondered if Paul Revere had really said those famous words.

_____ 5. Leeza dropped the box, and two plates broke with crashing sound.

_____ 6. Myna likes mysteries, but her brother prefers westerns.

_____ 7. We can have lunch now, or we can wait for Raphael.

_____ 8. The alligator jumped back into the river after he had been lying in the sunshine.

_____ 9. The bus reached our street twenty minutes late.

_____ 10. Ahmed found his shoes, but his socks are still missing.

_____ 11. A woman in California got into *The Guinness Book of World Records* because she blew a 22-inch bubble.

_____ 12. I have worn contact lenses ever since I realized I had bad vision.

_____ 13. We can swim, or I can row us to the island.

_____ 14. Kalila arrived early, but the others came much later in the day.

_____ 15. Although my parents dislike that band's music, they will still allow me to attend the concert.

_____ 16. We will attend tomorrow's conference unless our boss decides against it.

_____ 17. You are breaking the law in Kentucky if you carry an ice cream cone in your pocket.

_____ 18. I painted my room yellow, but red is my favorite color.

# CHAPTER 22  Clauses Review

**EXERCISE** Select the term that correctly identifies each sentence or group of words in the following paragraph.

My family likes to pick apples in October. **(1)** <u>When there is a sunny day</u>, we all pile into the car and drive to the apple orchard, **(2)** <u>which is located several miles outside of town</u>. **(3)** <u>Everyone enjoys the drive because the countryside is so pretty</u>. **(4)** <u>We especially admire the changing colors of the autumn leaves</u>. However, we also like seeing the cows and horses **(5)** <u>that are out grazing in the fields</u>. **(6)** <u>After</u> we arrive, we borrow a ladder from the big red barn. **(7)** <u>Although I usually pick apples that I can reach from the ground, my brother likes using the ladder to reach apples that are up high</u>. We pick all different kinds—red and green, sweet and sour, big and small. **(8)** <u>It is so much fun!</u> **(9)** <u>Even though</u> we all enjoy picking apples, **(10)** <u>we especially enjoy eating them</u>. **(11)** <u>They are delicious to eat just as they are, yet they're also great for homemade pie, applesauce, apple jelly, and more</u>.

_____ 1. A  independent clause
       B  adjectival clause
       C  adverbial clause
       D  simple sentence

_____ 2. A  adjectival clause
       B  adverbial clause
       C  independent clause
       D  simple sentence

_____ 3. A  simple sentence
       B  compound sentence
       C  independent clause
       D  complex sentence

_____ 4. A  compound sentence
       B  simple sentence
       C  complex sentence
       D  independent clause

_____ 5. A  adjectival clause
       B  adverbial clause
       C  independent clause
       D  simple sentence

_____ 6. A  independent clause
       B  subordinating conjunction
       C  subordinate clause
       D  adjectival clause

_____ 7. A  compound sentence
       B  independent clause
       C  complex sentence
       D  simple sentence

_____ 8. A  compound sentence
       B  independent clause
       C  complex sentence
       D  simple sentence

_____ 9. A  subordinating conjunction
       B  independent clause
       C  adverbial clause
       D  adjectival clause

_____ 10. A  subordinate clause
        B  independent clause
        C  simple sentence
        D  adjectival clause

_____ 11. A  compound sentence
        B  complex sentence
        C  simple sentence
        D  independent clause

Name _____ Date _____

## CHAPTER 23 — Sentence Fragments

**[23A]** A **sentence fragment** is a group of words punctuated as a sentence that does not express a complete thought.

> **EXERCISE** Write S if the group of words is a sentence or F if it is a sentence fragment.

_____ 1. Cleared a space on the table for her pile of books.

_____ 2. The two leads during the last act of the musical.

_____ 3. Indiana is a beautiful state in the middle of the country.

_____ 4. Hated waking up on cold mornings in the middle of the winter.

_____ 5. Some penguins live near the equator.

_____ 6. Among the branches of trees and shrubs in North America is.

_____ 7. Toad skins are rough and dry.

_____ 8. Five strong tribes of Iroquois Indians in one league.

_____ 9. The oldest of all games played with a ball and a stick.

_____ 10. We rested in a shady spot under a pine tree.

_____ 11. Fills the dough with bubbles.

_____ 12. The highest point on the surface of Earth.

_____ 13. Began before the crowd took their seats in the stadium.

_____ 14. Tankers carry liquid cargo.

_____ 15. The ninth month of the year is September.

_____ 16. Spend all of their time on the ocean floor.

_____ 17. A small tropical monkey with a large tail.

_____ 18. The couple, from the very first step of the dance.

# CHAPTER 23  Sentence Fragments

**EXERCISE** Rewrite each sentence fragment to make it a complete sentence.

1. Played guitar at the concert.

2. The highest peak in the Rocky Mountains.

3. Scored a home run in the final inning of the baseball game.

4. Ran up the stairs to the third floor.

5. Farmers on both sides of the Rio Grande.

6. The upper and lower parts of the shoe.

7. A sports magazine in the library.

8. Sat quietly in the back of the auditorium for an hour.

9. A floppy-eared puppy with large, sad eyes.

10. Spoke to the team after the game.

11. A nation without a king or some other monarch as leader.

Name _____  Date _____

# CHAPTER 23  Phrase Fragments

**[23B]** A **phrase fragment** is a group of words standing alone without a subject or a verb.

**EXERCISE A** Choose whether each group of words is a phrase fragment or a sentence.

_____ 1. At the corner near the school.
  A  phrase fragment
  B  sentence

_____ 2. We waited at the bus stop.
  A  phrase fragment
  B  sentence

_____ 3. In the basement, we found an old bicycle.
  A  phrase fragment
  B  sentence

_____ 4. Walking down a crowded street at rush hour.
  A  phrase fragment
  B  sentence

_____ 5. To notice the boy in the green jacket.
  A  phrase fragment
  B  sentence

_____ 6. Saturn has a moon.
  A  phrase fragment
  B  sentence

**EXERCISE B** Rewrite the following phrase fragments to make them complete sentences.

7. At the end of the final song on the CD.
   _____

8. On the edge of the lake.
   _____

9. To keep the sun out of your eyes.
   _____

10. Underneath the dining room table.
    _____

11. Eating ice cream cones.
    _____

12. To learn how to water ski.
    _____

# CHAPTER 23  Clause Fragments

**[23C]** A **clause fragment** is a subordinate clause punctuated as a sentence.

> **EXERCISE** Write S if the group of words is a complete sentence or CF if the group of words is a clause fragment.

_____ 1. Because we need to be at school on time.

_____ 2. We went shopping so that we could get our new supplies.

_____ 3. Who can answer the questions?

_____ 4. Is this the answer that we should write on the paper?

_____ 5. Since he was a little boy.

_____ 6. My dog likes to run in circles.

_____ 7. Barney spent many years perfecting his French accent.

_____ 8. Who is my favorite uncle.

_____ 9. Wild mustangs are beautiful.

_____ 10. Which was going to be my answer.

_____ 11. Which do you prefer?

_____ 12. People usually want to believe the best.

_____ 13. Although they went to Nairobi.

_____ 14. During the Bronze Age, meteorites were the only source of iron.

_____ 15. Will you travel by subway or take a bus?

_____ 16. Joe phones his best friend every evening.

_____ 17. Until the writer arrives at the bookstore.

_____ 18. Unless she writes many famous books.

Name _____  Date _____

## CHAPTER 23  Run-on Sentences

**[23D]** A **run-on sentence** is two or more sentences that are written together and separated by a comma or no punctuation at all.

> **EXERCISE** Write *sentence* if the group of words is a complete and correct sentence. If the group of words is a run-on sentence, rewrite it to make it correct.

1. Coyotes are nomads, they usually travel alone.

2. Alaska is our largest state it has the least number of people.

3. Opossums move very slowly and are caught easily.

4. Ostrich eggs are huge and weigh about three pounds each.

5. Some foods are canned, others are frozen or dried.

6. Pigs are very intelligent they can be taught tricks.

7. As popcorn explodes, steam escapes into the air.

8. Rita changed the bicycle tire Nan helped.

9. Strawberry seeds are on the outside of each berry.

10. My ear is sore, I'll visit the clinic.

11. People breathe oxygen, fish do too.

12. A football team can score points in four ways.

Name _____  Date _____

# CHAPTER 23  Sentence Fragments and Run-ons Review

**EXERCISE** Write the letter of the best way to write each underlined group of words. If the underlined words contain no error, choose D.

(1) Ticks are <u>very patient, they may be</u> the most patient creatures on the earth. (2) Some bugs fly or hop from <u>one animal to another. For a tasty meal.</u> (3) <u>A tick, however, will cling to a bush or a blade of grass for as long as two years.</u> (4) It just <u>waits patiently, it hopes an animal</u> will pass nearby. (5) A tick bite can cause <u>several diseases they include Lyme disease and tularemia.</u> (6) <u>Fever is often a symptom of such a disease or infection.</u> As an animal brushes against the spot (7) <u>where the tick is waiting. The tick climbs</u> aboard. (8) <u>Sometimes the tick grabs and misses, what happens then?</u> It (9) <u>climbs back. Onto the bush or blade of grass</u> and starts its wait all over again.

_____ 1. **A** very patient they may be
   **B** very patient. They may be
   **C** very patient, they may be,
   **D** No error

_____ 2. **A** one animal to another for a tasty meal.
   **B** One animal to another. For a tasty meal.
   **C** one animal to another, for a tasty meal.
   **D** No error

_____ 3. **A** A tick, however. Will cling to a bush or a blade of grass for as long as two years
   **B** A tick, however, will cling. To a bush or a blade of grass for as long as two years
   **C** A tick, however, will cling to a bush or a blade of grass, it will cling for as long as two years
   **D** No error

_____ 4. **A** waits patiently. Since it hopes an animal
   **B** waits patiently it hopes an animal
   **C** waits patiently and hopes an animal
   **D** No error

_____ 5. **A** several diseases, they include Lyme disease and tularemia.
   **B** several diseases, including Lyme disease and tularemia.
   **C** Several diseases they include Lyme disease and tularemia.
   **D** No error

_____ 6. **A** Fever is often a symptom. Of such a disease or infection.
   **B** Fever is often. A symptom of such a disease or infection.
   **C** Fever is often a symptom, it is a symptom of such a disease or infection.
   **D** No error

_____ 7. **A** where the tick is waiting, the tick climbs
   **B** where the tick is waiting the tick climbs
   **C** where the tick is waiting. The tick climbs.
   **D** No error

_____ 8. **A** Sometimes the tick grabs and misses what happens then?
   **B** Sometimes the tick grabs and misses. What happens then?
   **C** Sometimes the tick. Grabs and misses, but what happens then?
   **D** No error

_____ 9. **A** climbs back, onto the bush or blade of grass
   **B** climbs back onto the bush. Or blade of grass
   **C** climbs back onto the bush or blade of grass
   **D** No error

# CHAPTER 24  The Principal Parts of Verbs

**[24A]** The **principal parts** of a verb are the present, the present participle, the past, and the past participle.

**EXERCISE** Select the correct verb form in each sentence.

_____ 1. Tim _____ a wonderful speech at the assembly.
    **A** made
    **B** have made
    **C** make

_____ 2. Many immigrants have _____ their customs with them.
    **A** bring
    **B** bringing
    **C** brought

_____ 3. The jungle _____ no trace of the ancient city.
    **A** leave
    **B** has leave
    **C** left

_____ 4. He has _____ the same thing before.
    **A** says
    **B** say
    **C** said

_____ 5. Engineers have _____ many safety devices on cars.
    **A** put
    **B** putting
    **C** has put

_____ 6. The balloons _____ all over the ballroom.
    **A** bursting
    **B** bursted
    **C** burst

_____ 7. I _____ the telephone ring only once.
    **A** let
    **B** letting
    **C** would letting

_____ 8. Our coach _____ us the swan dive.
    **A** teached
    **B** has teached
    **C** taught

_____ 9. Has he _____ anything to you?
    **A** says
    **B** said
    **C** saying

_____ 10. Our debating team has _____ all previous records.
    **A** break
    **B** broken
    **C** breaking

_____ 11. The campers _____ the campsite clean and neat.
    **A** left
    **B** leaving
    **C** leave

_____ 12. No one _____ for five minutes.
    **A** speak
    **B** spoke
    **C** speaking

# CHAPTER 24 — The Principal Parts of Verbs

**EXERCISE** Rewrite the following sentences, replacing incorrect verb forms with correct verb forms. If a sentence needs no change, write *correct*.

1. After a short discussion, we chose a list of candidates.

2. Kelsey had stole the ball from Paul and ran with it.

3. Has Pete chose the members of the first team?

4. That dog has taken one of my best shoes.

5. The jet has broke the sound barrier twice.

6. Last night, one of our pipes freeze.

7. Lou brung me here in his pickup truck.

8. The soccer game begun right on schedule.

9. The high wind blew the two sailing ships off course.

10. For several years, we have grew our own tomatoes.

11. The fire alarm has rung twice this morning.

12. Wes rung the doorbell and waited nervously.

Name _____  Date _____

## CHAPTER 24 Regular Verbs

**[24A.1]** A **regular verb** forms its past and past participle by adding *–ed* or *–d* to the present.

> **EXERCISE** Identify each underlined regular verb by writing *present*, *present participle*, *past*, or *past participle* on the line provided.

_____  1. Talk to your Dad about your history homework.

_____  2. Mom knitted me a new scarf.

_____  3. I have added these numbers three times, and I still don't have the answer.

_____  4. Dad is dividing the pie among the three of us.

_____  5. Sharon worried that we would be late.

_____  6. Run to that next marker.

_____  7. The twins are crying for their lost dog.

_____  8. Pay for the yearbook with cash or a check.

_____  9. Mom has grabbed all of the squirt guns.

_____  10. I helped her study for the math test.

_____  11. Thomas is trying to have a positive attitude.

_____  12. If you end the game now, you can still be on time.

_____  13. I slipped on the ice.

_____  14. Use this chart to help you with the experiment.

_____  15. Robin Hood robbed from the rich and gave to the poor.

_____  16. I have liked vanilla ice cream all my life.

_____  17. Stan said, "Rap lightly on the door."

_____  18. Dylan has rubbed his elbow against the wall.

Name _____  Date _____

# CHAPTER 24  Regular Verbs

**EXERCISE** Write the correct regular verb form for each sentence.

_____  1. Samuel (flipping, flipped) through the magazine.

_____  2. Taylor is (pushes, pushing) the gate open.

_____  3. Percy has (asked, asking) for an ice cream cone.

_____  4. The moon (glowed, glowing) brightly in the sky.

_____  5. (Walk, walked) with me on the riverbank.

_____  6. We are (moving, moved) to a new house.

_____  7. Shelly has (pick, picked) three pounds of cherries.

_____  8. (Touching, Touch) the paint carefully.

_____  9. Kyle (printing, printed) his name at the top of the page.

_____  10. The worms have (crawled, crawl) across the sidewalk.

_____  11. My computer (crash, crashed) in the middle of my project.

_____  12. (Look, Looked) at this mess!

_____  13. John (dropping, dropped) the ball on the asphalt.

_____  14. Joanna is (laughing, laugh) at the joke.

_____  15. (Smiled, Smile) for the camera.

_____  16. William has (copying, copied) the notes from the board.

_____  17. I have (typed, type) this paper three times.

_____  18. The cat is (purr, purring) contentedly.

# CHAPTER 24  Irregular Verbs

**[24A.2]** An **irregular verb** does not form its past and past participle by adding *-ed* or *-d* to the present.

> **EXERCISE** Circle the correct irregular verb form in each of the following sentences.

1. Has anyone (saw, seen) my blue sweater with the white reindeer designs?
2. Ned has (broke, broken) our school record for the high jump.
3. Uncle Mel (drove, drived) a school bus during the winter last year.
4. Ms. Tracy has (chose, chosen) the best runner on the track team for the marathon.
5. Has John ever (did, done) this kind of work?
6. The deer (ran, run) into the clearing.
7. Have you ever (went, gone) to a rodeo?
8. I (began, begun) the chores after dinner.
9. The first bell (rang, rung) three minutes ago.
10. Has Nick ever (wore, worn) that shirt?
11. Jessica (drank, drunk) three glasses of water after the race.
12. Who (sang, sung) the solo in the musical?
13. Have you (wrote, written) a thank-you note?
14. Several porpoises (swam, swum) close to the boat.
15. George (do, did) a second ballot count after the election last Tuesday.
16. Have you ever (sing, sung) in the school choir?
17. I have never (eaten, eat) such tasty meatloaf as yours.
18. Michael must have (rode, ridden) to school with Lucia.

# CHAPTER 24 — Irregular Verbs

**EXERCISE** Rewrite the following sentences, replacing the underlined verb with the correct irregular verb form.

1. The mail <u>come</u> an hour ago.

2. Rehearsal has <u>began</u> without us.

3. I <u>worn</u> my heavy jacket to last Tuesday's meeting.

4. Who <u>written</u> the Gettysburg Address?

5. Karen has <u>swam</u> across the lake several times.

6. The bells have <u>rang</u>, announcing the new year.

7. Allen has <u>rided</u> horses for ten years.

8. Last weekend, we <u>drived</u> to Salem.

9. Who <u>make</u> this fruit salad for lunch?

10. No one <u>knowed</u> the name of the visitor.

11. My brother has <u>gave</u> me his catcher's mitt.

12. Everyone <u>brang</u> a swimsuit and a towel to last Sunday's picnic.

Name _____  Date _____

## CHAPTER 24  Six Problem Verbs

**EXERCISE** Choose the correct verb to fill in the blank.

_____ 1. Please _____ that book when you come to my house.
   A  bring
   B  take

_____ 2. _____ me this song.
   A  Learn
   B  Teach

_____ 3. Audrey _____ the children have a snack.
   A  left
   B  let

_____ 4. When do you _____ for your trip?
   A  leave
   B  let

_____ 5. Emmy _____ the class how to make a sock puppet.
   A  learned
   B  taught

_____ 6. Albert _____ cookies to our friend who lives across the street.
   A  is bringing
   B  is taking

_____ 7. Katja usually _____ us a newspaper in the morning.
   A  brings
   B  takes

_____ 8. Sophie _____ her lines very quickly.
   A  learns
   B  teaches

_____ 9. Mrs. Johnson _____ her class very well.
   A  learns
   B  teaches

_____ 10. Andy _____ for Alaska.
   A  is leaving
   B  is letting

_____ 11. I can't believe his mom _____ him go.
   A  is leaving
   B  is letting

_____ 12. Gabe _____ his speech for the debate.
   A  is teaching
   B  is learning

_____ 13. Mr. Benson _____ our art class this year.
   A  is learning
   B  is teaching

_____ 14. Stacy _____ the puppy to her veterinarian, whose office is on Clark Street.
   A  has taken
   B  has brought

| Name | Date |
|---|---|

## CHAPTER 24  Verb Tense

**[24B]** The time expressed by a verb is called the **tense** of the verb.
**[24B.1] Present tense** is used to express an action that is going on now.
**[24B.2] Past tense** expresses an action that already took place or was completed in the past.
**[24B.3] Future tense** is used to express an action that will take place in the future.
**[24B.4] Present perfect tense** expresses an action that was completed at some indefinite time in the past.
**[24B.5] Past perfect tense** expresses an action that took place before some other action.
**[24B.6] Future perfect tense** expresses an action that will take place before another future action or time.

> **EXERCISE** Label the tense of each underlined verb as *present, past, future, present perfect, past perfect*, or *future perfect*.

_____ 1. Maria <u>will choose</u> her favorite poem.

_____ 2. A filly <u>becomes</u> a mare at the age of five.

_____ 3. Debbie suddenly realized that she <u>had left</u> her flippers on the dock.

_____ 4. I think I <u>have met</u> you before.

_____ 5. Mom and Dad <u>will meet</u> you at the airport.

_____ 6. Roger Bannister <u>broke</u> the four-minute mile in 1954.

_____ 7. After Alex <u>had raked</u> the leaves, he put them in large plastic bags.

_____ 8. Dolphins <u>sleep</u> with one eye open at all times.

_____ 9. I <u>will ride</u> Brown Beauty tomorrow after school.

_____ 10. My cousin <u>has lived</u> in Omaha for three years.

_____ 11. The first wristwatch <u>appeared</u> as early as 1790.

_____ 12. By this time tomorrow, we <u>will have</u> learned half our lines.

_____ 13. In a few hours, snow <u>has covered</u> all the landscape within sight.

# CHAPTER 24  Verb Tense

**EXERCISE** Write each underlined verb in the tense that is indicated in parentheses.

_____ 1. Next semester, I <u>take</u> (*future*) art, gymnastics, and computer science.

_____ 2. By the close of school, I <u>drop</u> (*past perfect*) my glasses somewhere in the building.

_____ 3. Last summer, we <u>visit</u> (*past*) the Black Hills in South Dakota.

_____ 4. The language of Iceland <u>remain</u> (*present perfect*) unchanged since the twelfth century.

_____ 5. Today's heavy rains <u>end</u> (*future*) the recent drought.

_____ 6. The crew <u>paint</u> (*past*) the house in ten days.

_____ 7. By the end of the school year, I <u>complete</u> (*future perfect*) 30 credit hours.

_____ 8. In 1985, Pete Rose <u>break</u> (*past*) Ty Cobb's record of 4,191 base hits.

_____ 9. Linda <u>see</u> (*past perfect*) that movie before.

_____ 10. Most cats <u>sleep</u> (*present*) twenty hours each day.

_____ 11. Jill and Tony <u>write</u> (*present perfect*) a new song.

_____ 12. Tomorrow the sun <u>set</u> (*future*) over the bay.

_____ 13. Gene <u>send</u> (*past perfect*) only half of the invitations.

_____ 14. Darcy <u>save</u> (*present perfect*) enough money for a new MP3 player.

_____ 15. One thousand bees <u>make</u> (*present*) only one pound of honey during their entire lives.

_____ 16. By the end of the summer, Kate <u>earn</u> (*past perfect*) enough money for a new bicycle.

_____ 17. I <u>enjoy</u> (*present perfect*) the weather this fall.

## CHAPTER 24  Shifts in Tense

**[24B.8]** Avoid unnecessary shifts in tense within a sentence or within related sentences.

> **EXERCISE**  Write S if the sentence contains an unnecessary and incorrect shift in tense. If the sentence is correct, write C.

_____ 1. When I ride the horse for a few miles, my legs went numb.

_____ 2. Before you get on the bus, check your backpack.

_____ 3. When I finished the play, I find a rip in my costume.

_____ 4. Because I wasn't ready, I will not go on the trip.

_____ 5. Sam says that he has a new watch.

_____ 6. I told Myrtle that I needed new glasses.

_____ 7. Mrs. Costanza gave me a needle, and I fixed my costume quickly.

_____ 8. After John sang his song, he exited the stage.

_____ 9. By the time the sun came out, the children will leave for the park.

_____ 10. The new tenor will help our choir and gave us a lot to think about.

_____ 11. When Stewart tells his camping stories, we all listen.

_____ 12. After you finish the test, put your paper on the table.

_____ 13. Jenny will work with Armando, and I will help Tony.

_____ 14. Susan gave me her notes, but I did not need them.

_____ 15. Aaron says that he wants to practice.

_____ 16. When Mrs. Thomas checked our papers, she smiles.

_____ 17. Tom skated a few blocks, and his ankle goes out.

_____ 18. Dad baked the cake, but the guest never arrives.

_____ 19. Before you arrive at the gate, pick up your passport.

_____ 20. After we visited the zoo, we will ride on the train.

# CHAPTER 24  Progressive Verb Forms

**[24B.9]** The **progressive forms** of verbs are used to express continuing or ongoing action.

> **EXERCISE** Underline each verb phrase. Then label it as *present progressive, past progressive, future progressive, present perfect progressive, past perfect progressive,* or *future perfect progressive.*

_____ 1. This year, we have gone fishing three or four times.

_____ 2. Today we are hoping for clear skies.

_____ 3. The lions will be entering the ring in a few minutes.

_____ 4. The tigers are roaring loudly.

_____ 5. The trainer is pacing before the cage.

_____ 6. This morning, the lions were acting hungry.

_____ 7. This filter will be cleaning our water.

_____ 8. It seems the sun is setting later.

_____ 9. The hamburgers had been getting cold.

_____ 10. Kirk was practicing his fastball.

_____ 11. At the end of this summer, I will have been swimming for eight summers.

_____ 12. Meg has been collecting coins for a long time.

_____ 13. I have been talking to my parents about college.

_____ 14. We will be calling you from the station.

_____ 15. The Davidsons are raising golden retrievers.

_____ 16. I will be going to the mountains this summer.

_____ 17. Julio was talking to Mr. Rodriguez about the book fair.

_____ 18. Sherman will be running for president of the chess club.

Name _____  Date _____

# CHAPTER 24  Using Verbs Review

**EXERCISE** Read each sentence and write the letter of the word or group of words that belongs in the underlined space.

_____ 1. Last night, Jennifer _____ the roast to Jane's dinner party.
   A took
   B taked
   C will take
   D has taken

_____ 2. Melvin _____ Elissa a lovely bouquet of flowers yesterday.
   A brung
   B bringed
   C brang
   D brought

_____ 3. Many people have _____ the English Channel.
   A swam
   B swim
   C swum
   D swimmed

_____ 4. Check your tackle box before you _____ the dock.
   A left
   B leave
   C were leaving
   D have been leaving

_____ 5. My little brother accidentally _____ his dinner plate.
   A breaked
   B broke
   C breaking
   D broken

_____ 6. The sun went down, and I _____ up my gear.
   A packed
   B pack
   C will pack
   D will have packed

_____ 7. Many people have _____ themselves a foreign language.
   A learn
   B learned
   C teached
   D taught

_____ 8. Ellie has _____ to the park.
   A went
   B goed
   C gone
   D going

_____ 9. Jack has _____ his corn without butter or salt.
   A eat
   B eated
   C eaten
   D ate

_____ 10. When Robbie _____ his lines, he found a big bass.
   A checks
   B will check
   C will have been checking
   D was checking

_____ 11. Chris has _____ us our cameras.
   A brought
   B bring
   C taken
   D took

_____ 12. Kim _____ Spanish next summer.
   A learned
   B has learned
   C had learned
   D will be learning

Name _____  Date _____

# CHAPTER 25 — Identifying the Cases of Personal Pronouns

**[25A]** **Case** is the form of a noun or pronoun that indicates its use in the sentence.
**[25A.1]** The **nominative case** is used both for subjects and for predicate nominatives.
**[25A.3]** The **objective case** is used for direct objects, indirect objects, and objects of prepositions.
**[25A.4]** The **possessive case** is used to show ownership or possession.

> **EXERCISE** Identify the case of each underlined pronoun by writing *nominative*, *objective*, or *possessive* on the line provided.

_____  1. Are <u>they</u> your cousins?

_____  2. The shark devoured <u>its</u> prey.

_____  3. Will you go to the park with <u>me</u>?

_____  4. Rob and <u>he</u> are leaving.

_____  5. The principal called Brandon and <u>him</u> to the office.

_____  6. <u>She</u> will be going with us to the carnival.

_____  7. Where is <u>your</u> apartment?

_____  8. <u>Hers</u> is the best poem in the class.

_____  9. Please help <u>us</u> with our lines.

_____  10. <u>We</u> will be riding our bikes tomorrow.

_____  11. That one is <u>mine</u>.

_____  12. Where have <u>you</u> been?

_____  13. It will be hard to hear <u>them</u> if the sound system is down.

_____  14. <u>They</u> are the fastest members of the team.

_____  15. Shaun gave the baton to <u>him</u>.

_____  16. I can't believe the championship is <u>ours</u>.

# CHAPTER 25  Identifying the Cases of Personal Pronouns

**EXERCISE** Underline the pronoun in each of the following sentences. Write N for nominative, O for objective, or P for possessive on the blank.

_____ 1. <u>It</u> sat down and gave a mechanical bark.

_____ 2. Could the glove be <u>yours</u>?

_____ 3. Lavinia is going to the play with <u>her</u>.

_____ 4. <u>Her</u> voice is beautiful.

_____ 5. <u>They</u> will have to finish the game later.

_____ 6. Jason said Tom wanted to go with <u>you</u>.

_____ 7. After all, the book is <u>hers</u>.

_____ 8. Ellen went to <u>their</u> house for the weekend.

_____ 9. Dad threw the ball to <u>me</u>.

_____ 10. <u>You</u> should have seen Mom's face.

_____ 11. The cat licked <u>its</u> paw.

_____ 12. <u>Our</u> boat is very fast.

_____ 13. The orange scarf is <u>mine</u>.

_____ 14. Ron gave <u>her</u> a ticket.

_____ 15. Are <u>you</u> going to the circus?

_____ 16. Dad gave <u>you</u> three chances.

_____ 17. <u>They</u> want to win.

_____ 18. Gail gave <u>her</u> a pen.

# CHAPTER 25  Pronouns Used as Subjects

**EXERCISE** Choose the correct pronoun in each sentence.

_____ 1. Gini and _____ are looking for a ride to the picnic.
  A  he
  B  him
  C  us

_____ 2. Harry and _____ will arrive before four o'clock.
  A  me
  B  I
  C  us

_____ 3. Are Mei–Ling and _____ singing a duet?
  A  she
  B  her
  C  me

_____ 4. Bob and _____ worked at the outdoor market yesterday.
  A  he
  B  us
  C  me

_____ 5. Have Joanne and _____ played tennis together?
  A  him
  B  us
  C  he

_____ 6. Last Saturday, Marcia and _____ all celebrated our birthdays together.
  A  us
  B  we
  C  them

_____ 7. Peggy and _____ are going to the movies.
  A  I
  B  me
  C  her

_____ 8. _____ have not been absent this year.
  A  Me
  B  They
  C  Them

_____ 9. Alan and _____ baked a strawberry-rhubarb pie.
  A  her
  B  she
  C  me

_____ 10. Eva and _____ are going in the same costumes.
  A  me
  B  us
  C  I

_____ 11. Ricky and _____ dance very well together.
  A  me
  B  she
  C  her

_____ 12. Did _____ ever get to the top of Pikes Peak?
  A  him
  B  me
  C  she

_____ 13. _____ worked in Webster's Garage last summer.
  A  He
  B  Her
  C  Them

_____ 14. Rachel and _____ are good skaters.
  A  me
  B  I
  C  them

# CHAPTER 25  Pronouns Used as Predicate Nominatives

**[25A.2]** A **predicate nominative** is a word that follows a linking verb and identifies or renames the subject.

**EXERCISE** Circle the correct pronoun to complete each sentence.

1. The last two into the pool were Joe and (me, **I**, him).

2. The man in the blue jacket is (them, him, **he**).

3. The real heroes of the game were (**they**, them, us).

4. Is that (her, **she**, him) at the front door?

5. The first one with an empty plate was (him, **he**, me).

6. That baby on Grandmother's lap is (me, **it**, I).

7. The dangerous animals are (**they**, them, us).

8. The safest driver in the class is (her, **she**, me).

9. Is that (her, them, **she**) in the wet suit?

10. The cutest monkeys are (**they**, them, us).

11. Surprise! The finalists in the tournament are (me, him, **they**).

12. The Cubs fans in the family are Fred and (**I**, me, her).

13. The woman with the black suitcase is (her, **she**, him).

14. The referee at tonight's game will be (him, her, **he**).

15. The only T-shirts for sale were for (they, **them**, us).

16. The quarterback this Saturday will be either George or (me, **I**, us).

Name _____   Date _____

## CHAPTER 25  Pronouns Used as Direct and Indirect Objects

**EXERCISE** Write the correct pronoun for each sentence.

_____ 1. The coach gave Jake and (me, I, he) some good pointers.

_____ 2. Our parents gave (we, he, us) tickets to the circus.

_____ 3. Did you invite Annie and (he, we, him) to your party?

_____ 4. The announcer called Mark and (I, me, she) to the stage.

_____ 5. The bus dropped Martha and (her, she, he) at the corner.

_____ 6. Ellen showed (he, him, we) photographs of her entire family.

_____ 7. The skunk gave Jon and (me, I, she) a real scare.

_____ 8. The driver told Kay and (they, we, them) about the race.

_____ 9. Please pass Stan and (I, me, she) the orange juice.

_____ 10. We saw Aretha and (he, him, she) on the plane to Atlanta.

_____ 11. Give Patty and (her, she, he) the prizes.

_____ 12. Ella and Sally took my sister and (I, he, me) for a boat ride.

_____ 13. Ms. Abels gave Joe and (I, she, him) some lemonade.

_____ 14. The clown pulled Pat and (her, she, I) into the ring.

_____ 15. Mr. Jackson called my brother and (them, they, we) to his office.

_____ 16. June showed (her, he, I) and Paul pictures of the canyon.

Name _____   Date _____

# CHAPTER 25  Pronouns Used as Objects of Prepositions

**EXERCISE A** Choose the correct form of the pronoun in each sentence.

_____ 1. Mr. Peters sat between Myrtle and _____.
   A  I
   B  me
   C  she

_____ 2. The conductor just pointed at you and _____.
   A  me
   B  he
   C  she

_____ 3. Dad made these sandwiches for Stan and _____.
   A  they
   B  he
   C  them

_____ 4. So far, I have written only to Terry and _____.
   A  she
   B  her
   C  he

_____ 5. Bill sat in front of Ben and _____.
   A  I
   B  me
   C  he

_____ 6. The Gosnells took me with Claire and _____ to the rink.
   A  they
   B  we
   C  them

**EXERCISE B** Complete each sentence by writing an appropriate pronoun.

7. Between you and _____, couldn't we have walked to school?

8. Sit in back between Rosa and _____.

9. Did you make this dessert specially for Tim and _____?

10. The money will be given to the Byrds and _____.

11. Will you climb Mt. McKinley with the Lees and _____?

12. I will sit near Nancy and _____.

13. Jack was sitting between Paul and _____.

# CHAPTER 25  The Possessive Case

**EXERCISE** If the underlined pronoun is in the wrong case, write it correctly. If it is in the correct case, write *correct*.

_____  1. That coat is <u>mine</u> cousin's.

_____  2. Which bike is <u>yours</u>?

_____  3. <u>Theirs</u> family is going to the Bahamas this winter.

_____  4. I got <u>my</u> new glasses last weekend.

_____  5. Are those DVDs <u>hers</u>?

_____  6. <u>Ours</u> next play will be in two weeks.

_____  7. Where is <u>your</u> radio?

_____  8. <u>His</u> bird sings all the time.

_____  9. <u>Mine</u> bird is cleaning his feathers.

_____ 10. Sharon had hoped that <u>hers</u> bird would learn to whistle.

_____ 11. That house looks like <u>ours</u>.

_____ 12. It looks as if the prize will be <u>theirs</u>.

_____ 13. <u>Theirs</u> daughter won a scholarship.

_____ 14. <u>Hers</u> brother is very nice.

_____ 15. The boat with the red trim is <u>his</u>.

_____ 16. Which one is <u>your</u>?

_____ 17. Susie likes <u>her</u> new teacher.

_____ 18. <u>Yours</u> flowers are looking good.

# CHAPTER 25  Possessive Pronoun or Contraction?

**EXERCISE** Choose the possessive pronoun or contraction to complete each sentence.

____ 1. Where is _____ math book?
   A  your
   B  you're

____ 2. _____ going to rain tomorrow.
   A  Its
   B  It's

____ 3. _____ is this canned food?
   A  Who's
   B  Whose

____ 4. _____ going to the concert?
   A  Who's
   B  Whose

____ 5. _____ are the prettiest flowers in the garden.
   A  Hers
   B  Her's

____ 6. _____ on the judging panel?
   A  Who's
   B  Whose

____ 7. _____ car just drove up.
   A  Their
   B  They're

____ 8. _____ the perfect person for this job!
   A  Your
   B  You're

____ 9. _____ their sponsor for the charity race?
   A  Who's
   B  Whose

____ 10. My cat doesn't like _____ new bed.
   A  its
   B  it's

____ 11. _____ a present for you in the den.
   A  Theirs
   B  There's

____ 12. _____ is this invitation to the dance?
   A  Who's
   B  Whose

____ 13. _____ the lead actor in that movie?
   A  Who's
   B  Whose

____ 14. The car with the rusty fender is _____.
   A  ours
   B  our's

Name _____  Date _____

## CHAPTER 25 — Pronouns and Their Antecedents

**[25C]** A pronoun and its **antecedent**, the word that a pronoun refers to or replaces, must agree in number and gender.

> **EXERCISE** Write an appropriate pronoun that agrees with the underlined antecedent in each sentence.

1. Jack put on _____ costume.

2. At the last moment, John remembered _____ sunglasses.

3. I did clean and oil _____ bicycle chain.

4. Betty bought a pen and pencil set for _____ brother.

5. After the downpour they checked _____ rain gauge.

6. Anna invited us to _____ house for dinner.

7. Do the bicycle riders have _____ helmets on?

8. Does a long-haired cat keep _____ fur clean?

9. Pete brought _____ catcher's mitt to school.

10. A tiger enjoys raw meat for _____ dinner.

11. Do the hikers know _____ way to the falls?

12. The howler monkey greeted the sunrise with _____ howl.

13. This amusement park has _____ own bus line.

14. The MacKenzies are trading _____ car.

15. Randy made a swing for _____ younger sister.

Name _____ Date _____

# CHAPTER 25  Indefinite Pronouns as Antecedents

**EXERCISE** Circle the pronoun that agrees with the underlined antecedent in each sentence.

1. <u>Each</u> of the chipmunks was carrying peanuts in (their, his, its) cheeks.

2. <u>Neither</u> of the boys had brought (his, their, its) books.

3. <u>One</u> of the eagles broke (his, her, its) wing.

4. Did you ask <u>either</u> of the girls for (their, his, her) decision?

5. Only a <u>few</u> brought (her, his, their) compasses.

6. <u>Each</u> of the poems will have (his, their, its) place on the bulletin board.

7. <u>Each</u> of the cats has (its, their, his) own dish in the kitchen.

8. <u>Everyone</u> on the men's soccer team wore (his, her, its) T-shirt.

9. <u>Several</u> of the campers had (his, her, their) own first-aid kits.

10. <u>Each</u> of the girls contributed (her, his, their) share.

11. <u>Everyone</u> on the girls' team won (his, her, their) letter.

12. <u>One</u> of the girls forgot (their, his, her) tennis racket.

13. <u>Each</u> of the pines was three feet from (its, their, his) neighbor.

14. <u>Many</u> of the drivers serviced (his, her, their) own cars.

Name _____  Date _____

# CHAPTER 25  Unclear or Missing Antecedents

**EXERCISE** Write I for each antecedent that is missing or unclear. Write C for each antecedent that is used correctly.

_____ 1. I don't like the snorkel equipment because you are having trouble.

_____ 2. Joey likes the ocean because he can go surfing.

_____ 3. At the end of our vacation, it felt good.

_____ 4. Ted likes the beach because I get to look for shells.

_____ 5. Donna's face was red, but now it has faded.

_____ 6. Vera got a new bathing suit so that she can swim better.

_____ 7. Jonathan and Billy went to his house.

_____ 8. Kerry emptied her bucket and let it fall onto the sand.

_____ 9. I have never tried a back flip, but I still enjoy diving.

_____ 10. Brenda and Gina couldn't finish her homework.

_____ 11. Joanie hasn't found its owner yet.

_____ 12. Richard has paid your field trip money.

_____ 13. Roberta has left the water on in her bathroom.

_____ 14. The students must turn in my paperwork.

_____ 15. You must carry your backpack at all times.

_____ 16. The area is famous for your changes in the weather.

_____ 17. Anne writes her own mystery stories.

_____ 18. Todd has a brother, and she is fifteen.

_____ 19. One story has her setting in Ireland.

_____ 20. Tranh wants a story to keep her guessing.

# CHAPTER 25  Using Pronouns Review

**EXERCISE** Read the passage and write the letter of the word that belongs in each underlined space.

On Tuesday Joanne and **(1)** _____ took a picnic to Pickins Park. Joanne told **(2)** _____ that **(3)** _____ and Ivan are playing a four-hands piano piece at the fair this year. Last year's blue ribbon went to Joanne and **(4)** _____, so I'm sure **(5)** _____ will do well again this year. I am really hoping, though, that the blue ribbon will be **(6)** _____ and Gretchen's. Gretchen and **(7)** _____ are going to perform a song and dance routine that **(8)** _____ have been practicing for months. "**(9)** _____ going to be so impressed," I told my mom and dad. Hopefully the judges will like **(10)** _____ performance. However, I'll be happy for whoever gets the ribbon because contests aren't only about who wins; **(11)** _____ also about having fun along the way.

_____ 1. **A** I
　　**B** me
　　**C** mine
　　**D** my

_____ 2. **A** I
　　**B** me
　　**C** mine
　　**D** my

_____ 3. **A** she
　　**B** her
　　**C** her's
　　**D** hers

_____ 4. **A** he
　　**B** his
　　**C** him
　　**D** theirs

_____ 5. **A** us
　　**B** it
　　**C** them
　　**D** they

_____ 6. **A** I
　　**B** me
　　**C** mine
　　**D** my

_____ 7. **A** I
　　**B** me
　　**C** mine
　　**D** my

_____ 8. **A** us
　　**B** ours
　　**C** we
　　**D** them

_____ 9. **A** You
　　**B** You're
　　**C** Your
　　**D** You's

_____ 10. **A** their
　　**B** its
　　**C** his
　　**D** our

_____ 11. **A** they're
　　**B** their
　　**C** they
　　**D** there's

Name _____  Date _____

## CHAPTER 26  Number

**[26A]** A verb must agree with its subject in number.

> **EXERCISE** Write S if the underlined subject is singular or P if it is plural.

_____ 1. The <u>chef</u> diced the potato by hand.

_____ 2. At dinner <u>they</u> lit the candles on the table.

_____ 3. <u>Joe</u> caught the ball in his mitt.

_____ 4. After school <u>we</u> work as volunteers at the hospital.

_____ 5. Most <u>people</u> in China eat with chopsticks.

_____ 6. This <u>truck</u> has eight wheels.

_____ 7. <u>Anne</u> enjoys her work in the cafeteria.

_____ 8. During the hike <u>she</u> led the way to the top of the cliffs.

_____ 9. <u>Chicago</u> is on the shores of Lake Michigan.

_____ 10. <u>Mushrooms</u> grow best in cool, dark places.

_____ 11. <u>It</u> is my favorite game.

_____ 12. <u>Children</u> love to play outdoors.

_____ 13. <u>I</u> can run, skate, climb, and hike.

_____ 14. His <u>friends</u> join him after school.

_____ 15. A <u>mouse</u> can make a great pet.

_____ 16. The <u>twins</u> have two bicycles in their garage.

_____ 17. <u>Students</u> play on the playground at recess.

_____ 18. <u>We</u> do our best when we play a soccer game.

_____ 19. The <u>players</u> have new uniforms.

_____ 20. This <u>tomato</u> is delicious.

Name_____  Date_____

# CHAPTER 26  Number

**EXERCISE** Write the underlined verbs from the sentences below in the appropriate column of the chart.

1. Roots <u>serve</u> as anchors for plants.
2. Many plants <u>have</u> underground roots.
3. However, some roots <u>climb</u> on trees or walls.
4. Poison ivy <u>has</u> such roots.
5. People <u>eat</u> many kinds of roots.
6. A carrot <u>is</u> one kind of root.
7. Beets <u>are</u> another kind.
8. Roots <u>thrive</u> in almost all gardens.
9. A banyan tree <u>looks</u> odd.
10. At first its roots <u>grow</u> in the air.
11. Eventually, each root <u>reaches</u> the ground.

|     | Singular Verbs | Plural Verbs |
| --- | --- | --- |
| 1.  |     |     |
| 2.  |     |     |
| 3.  |     |     |
| 4.  |     |     |
| 5.  |     |     |
| 6.  |     |     |
| 7.  |     |     |
| 8.  |     |     |
| 9.  |     |     |
| 10. |     |     |
| 11. |     |     |

Name _____  Date _____

## CHAPTER 26 Singular and Plural Subjects

**[26A.1]** A **singular subject** takes a singular verb. A **plural subject** takes a plural verb.

> **EXERCISE** Circle the verb that agrees with the underlined subject in each sentence.

1. My <u>pen</u> (write, writes) in three different colors.

2. The <u>boats</u> (sails, sail) across the lake.

3. These <u>candles</u> (melts, melt) when lit.

4. <u>Flowers</u> (grow, grows) in spring.

5. Tall <u>buildings</u> (sway, sways) in the wind.

6. <u>Skyscrapers</u> (soar, soars) into the sky.

7. A tall <u>building</u> (takes, take) up little valuable land.

8. Instead, <u>they</u> (rise, rises) many stories into the air.

9. <u>Elevators</u> (carries, carry) people to the upper floors.

10. Often a skyscraper's <u>roof</u> (contains, contain) an observation platform.

11. <u>Tourists</u> (enjoy, enjoys) the view from the top.

12. A city's <u>skyline</u> (change, changes) with the addition of new buildings.

13. Each city <u>skyline</u> (have, has) its own unique appearance.

14. No two <u>cities</u> (look, looks) alike from a distance.

# CHAPTER 26  Singular and Plural Subjects

**EXERCISE** Write the correct verb for each sentence on the line provided.

(1) In summer caterpillars (lives/live) everywhere. (2) They (crawl/crawls) through every neighborhood. (3) These leaf chompers (appears/appear) in all shapes and colors. (4) They each (looks/look) different. (5) Eventually, every caterpillar (turns/turn) into a moth or a butterfly. (6) A caterpillar (have/has) many enemies. (7) Ground beetles (attacks/attack) them on the ground. (8) Praying mantises (snatches/snatch) them from leaves. (9) Their most dangerous enemy, however, (is/are) birds. (10) A bird (eats/eat) dozens of caterpillars every day.

1. _____
2. _____
3. _____
4. _____
5. _____
6. _____
7. _____
8. _____
9. _____
10. _____

# CHAPTER 26  Verb Phrases

**[26B]** Helping verbs, contractions, interrupting words, and inverted order can lead to agreement problems.

**[26B.1]** The first helping verb must agree in number with the subject.

**EXERCISE** Choose the correct helping verb in each sentence.

_____ 1. Lemons _____ grown in Florida.
  A  is
  B  are

_____ 2. Yes, a penguin _____ have feathers on its body.
  A  do
  B  does

_____ 3. That chimney _____ look very old.
  A  does
  B  do

_____ 4. The glass house _____ built by Phillip Johnson.
  A  was
  B  were

_____ 5. Some caterpillars _____ sleep during the day.
  A  does
  B  do

_____ 6. Certain seals _____ remained under water for twenty minutes.
  A  has
  B  have

_____ 7. The Green Mountains _____ located in Vermont.
  A  are
  B  is

_____ 8. Mako sharks _____ attack anything.
  A  do
  B  does

_____ 9. Rita _____ lived here for five years.
  A  has
  B  have

_____ 10. Dogsleds _____ used in parts of Canada.
  A  are
  B  is

_____ 11. Bats _____ hanging from the cave roof.
  A  was
  B  were

_____ 12. The average American _____ eat about nine pounds of turkey each year.
  A  do
  B  does

_____ 13. Some animals _____ grown flippers in place of feet.
  A  have
  B  has

_____ 14. The hikers _____ sitting on top of the hill.
  A  were
  B  was

_____ 15. The beetle _____ chewing our best rose bush.
  A  were
  B  was

_____ 16. China _____ leading the world in rice production.
  A  was
  B  were

# CHAPTER 26 Agreement with Contractions

**[26B.2]** The verb part of a contraction must agree in number with the subject.

**EXERCISE** Write the correct contraction to complete each sentence.

_____ 1. James (doesn't, don't) care much about soccer.

_____ 2. (Wasn't, Weren't) you set for that broad jump?

_____ 3. Our cousins in Ohio (doesn't, don't) often visit us.

_____ 4. (Wasn't, Weren't) those birds unusual?

_____ 5. There (isn't, aren't) many prizes left.

_____ 6. Some guests (isn't, aren't) coming tonight.

_____ 7. (Hasn't, Haven't) anyone seen my sunglasses?

_____ 8. Eddie and Ellis (hasn't, haven't) arrived yet.

_____ 9. (Isn't, Aren't) a fork missing?

_____ 10. Julie and Joan (doesn't, don't) know our address.

_____ 11. The girls and their aunt (wasn't, weren't) very excited about the trip.

_____ 12. Many floats (isn't, aren't) ready for the parade.

_____ 13. (Doesn't, Don't) the music sound familiar?

_____ 14. The monkeys (hasn't, haven't) seen the new tire swing.

_____ 15. Terry and Beth (wasn't, weren't) going on vacation.

_____ 16. (Wasn't, Weren't) you the winner of the relay race?

_____ 17. The lamp (doesn't, don't) look good with that chair.

_____ 18. I (hasn't, haven't) ever seen the Grand Canyon.

_____ 19. Wolves (doesn't, don't) always howl.

Name _____ Date _____

## CHAPTER 26  Interrupting Words

**[26B.3]** The agreement of a verb with its subject is not changed by any interrupting words.

**EXERCISE** Choose the correct verb for the underlined subject in each sentence.

_____ 1. Farmers in Costa Rica _____ machetes.
  A  use
  B  uses

_____ 2. The colors of the Canadian flag _____ red and white.
  A  are
  B  is

_____ 3. The plants in my window box _____ quickly.
  A  sprouts
  B  sprout

_____ 4. At one time the fur of squirrels _____ used for hats.
  A  was
  B  were

_____ 5. Many farmers in this area _____ cotton.
  A  grow
  B  grows

_____ 6. The feathers of a duck _____ waterproof.
  A  is
  B  are

_____ 7. The bats in this cave _____ upside down.
  A  hang
  B  hangs

_____ 8. The waters of the North Atlantic _____ many fish.
  A  contain
  B  contains

_____ 9. Small mammals, such as mice and birds, _____ frequent meals for snakes.
  A  are
  B  is

_____ 10. A pile of old clothes _____ dumped in the basement.
  A  was
  B  were

_____ 11. A tree beside the garage _____ sprouted new buds.
  A  have
  B  has

_____ 12. The termites in that nest _____ the queen.
  A  feeds
  B  feed

_____ 13. Rome in its early days _____ a small town.
  A  was
  B  were

_____ 14. The front teeth of a rodent _____ growing.
  A  keeps
  B  keep

_____ 15. A river with all its tributaries _____ called a river system.
  A  is
  B  are

_____ 16. This map of the United States _____ only major cities.
  A  show
  B  shows

# CHAPTER 26  Inverted Order

**[26B.4]** The subject and verb of an inverted sentence must agree in number.

**EXERCISE** Circle the verb that agrees with the underlined subject(s) in each sentence.

1. There (are, is) many <u>breeds</u> of dogs in the United States.

2. In the center ring (was, were) four <u>monkeys</u> on bicycles.

3. (Were, Was) any <u>sandwiches</u> left for me?

4. Here (are, is) some new <u>stamps</u> from the post office.

5. Under the ocean floor (are, is) many valuable <u>minerals</u>.

6. There (was, were) other <u>explorers</u> in the Americas before Christopher Columbus.

7. On the tops of many city buildings (are, is) falcon <u>nests</u>.

8. (Do, Does) <u>you</u> play softball often?

9. (Has, Have) <u>you</u> ever seen the inside of a submarine?

10. On the fire escape (sits, sit) two stray <u>cats</u>.

11. Into the meadow (hops, hop) the young <u>rabbit</u>.

12. Here (is, are) two <u>dishes</u> of salad.

13. Where (were, was) <u>Carmen</u> and <u>Jeanie</u> going?

14. There (was, were) two <u>pigeons</u> on my windowsill.

15. In the empty lot (live, lives) an <u>opossum</u>.

16. (Was, Were) <u>Sandy</u> ever in Alaska?

Name _____  Date _____

# CHAPTER 26  Compound Subjects

**[26C]** Compound subjects and collective nouns can cause agreement problems.
**[26C.1]** When subjects are joined by *and*, the verb is usually plural.
**[26C.2]** When subjects are joined by *or*, *either/or*, or *neither/nor*, the verb agrees with the closer subject.

**EXERCISE** Write the correct form of the verb in parentheses.

_____ 1. Bats and mice (live, lives) in this old barn.

_____ 2. Hannah and Kim (take, takes) the train.

_____ 3. Mount Washington and Mount Mitchell (soar, soars) more than 6,000 feet.

_____ 4. Pelicans and herons (feed, feeds) on fish.

_____ 5. Jade and agate (are, is) mined in Alaska.

_____ 6. Neither my brothers nor my sister (looks, look) like me.

_____ 7. Tina or Barbara (has, have) borrowed my pen.

_____ 8. Either Beyoncé or her brothers (plays, play) basketball with us.

_____ 9. Neither the umbrellas nor the tree (give, gives) us enough shade.

_____ 10. Either the president or his assistants (conduct, conducts) the meetings.

_____ 11. Either calculators or a computer (has, have) been purchased.

_____ 12. This trunk and those suitcases (have, has) traveled many miles.

_____ 13. Either Janice or Susan (is, are) her best friend.

_____ 14. Neither the terns nor the gulls (have, has) returned yet.

_____ 15. Either those high bushes or that tree (are, is) blocking the sunlight.

_____ 16. Strawberries and blueberries often (grow, grows) wild.

_____ 17. The scallop and the oyster (are, is) found from Maine to Florida.

_____ 18. Sandra or Frank (has, have) set the table.

_____ 19. Neither Meredith nor her dog (is, are) here.

_____ 20. A pen or two pencils (is, are) needed.

# CHAPTER 26  Compound Subjects

**EXERCISE** Write the correct verb for each sentence on the line provided.

(1) Both salt and other spices (help/helps) preserve food. (2) Meat or vegetables (is/are) sometimes preserved in salty water. (3) In the past, either deer or wild pigs (was/were) hung near fires to dry out and preserve the meat. (4) Today turkeys and sausage (are/is) cured in the same way.

(5) Before grocery stores were widespread, neither fruit nor fresh vegetables (were/was) available everywhere during the winter. (6) Apples and corn (was/were) stored in pioneer wagons. (7) Grains and roots (was/were) stored in cellars. (8) Now either freezers or a refrigerator (keep/keeps) food fresh. (9) Frozen meat and vegetables (is/are) sold in almost every store. (10) Canned and dried food (is/are) also available.

1. _____
2. _____
3. _____
4. _____
5. _____
6. _____
7. _____
8. _____
9. _____
10. _____

# CHAPTER 26 Collective Nouns

**[26C.3]** Use a singular verb with a collective noun subject that is thought of as a unit. Use a plural verb with a collective noun that is thought of as individuals.

**EXERCISE** Circle the verb that agrees with the collective noun subject in each sentence.

1. The band (is/are) playing at the graduation ceremony.
2. That bunch of carrots (looks/look) rotten.
3. The class (argues/argue) about how to vote for Student Council.
4. A cluster of students (is/are) standing by the cafeteria.
5. After the committee (meets/meet), we will know their decision.
6. The Massachusetts Colony (disagree/disagrees) with the king over British taxes.
7. The congregation (is/are) singing in tune this morning.
8. The crew (works/work) well together.
9. A crowd of students (has/have) gathered in the office.
10. The wolf packs (defends/defend) their own territories.
11. My family (works/work) together when things are tough.
12. A flock of crows (means/mean) trouble for farmers.
13. The group (is/are) not meeting today.
14. The cattle herd (was/were) thirsty after the stampede.
15. My mom's bowling league (is/are) winning the city championship.
16. The orchestra (tunes/tune) their instruments before each performance.
17. The school (disagrees/disagree) about the kind of dress code we should have.
18. The swarm of bees (buzzes/buzz) angrily when disturbed.

Name _____  Date _____

## CHAPTER 26  *You* and *I* as Subjects

**[26D.1]** *You* is always used with a plural verb even when *you* refers to one person.
**[26D.2]** *I* takes a plural verb unless it is used with the verbs *am* or *was*.

**EXERCISE A**  Write C if the underlined verb is correct or I if it is incorrect.

_____ 1. You <u>is</u> one of my best friends.

_____ 2. I <u>enjoys</u> fresh pears.

_____ 3. Yesterday, you <u>were</u> on the soccer field early.

_____ 4. I <u>was</u> on top of the ladder.

_____ 5. I <u>has</u> three pairs of clean socks.

_____ 6. You <u>are</u> the first speaker of the day.

_____ 7. You <u>plays</u> chess very well.

_____ 8. You <u>has</u> new glasses on today.

_____ 9. You sometimes <u>talk</u> too softly in class.

**EXERCISE B**  Circle the correct verb in each sentence.

10. I (is, was) at camp for two weeks in August.

11. I (am, are) the first person on board.

12. I (has, have) a pair of new skis.

13. I (like, likes) the color blue.

14. You (were, was) my first choice for class president.

15. You (play, plays) the piano very skillfully.

16. You (have, has) all of my books in that bag.

17. I (build, builds) models of ships.

18. Boys, you (work, works) very hard.

Name _____ Date _____

## CHAPTER 26 Indefinite Pronouns

**[26D.3]** A verb must agree in number with an indefinite pronoun used as a subject.

**EXERCISE** Choose the verb that agrees with the underlined subject in each sentence.

_____ 1. <u>Neither</u> of the sailors _____ on deck during the storm.
  **A** was
  **B** were

_____ 2. <u>Both</u> of the streets _____ one way.
  **A** are
  **B** is

_____ 3. <u>Few</u> on the swimming team _____ passed all their tests.
  **A** has
  **B** have

_____ 4. <u>Somebody</u> in your house _____ shutting all the windows.
  **A** is
  **B** are

_____ 5. <u>Few</u> of the eggs _____ cracked.
  **A** are
  **B** is

_____ 6. <u>Neither</u> of the faucets _____ leaking now.
  **A** are
  **B** is

_____ 7. <u>Someone</u> in the building _____ moving out.
  **A** is
  **B** are

_____ 8. <u>Both</u> of the dishes _____ cold.
  **A** are
  **B** is

_____ 9. <u>Each</u> of those birds _____ in our bird bath.
  **A** bathe
  **B** bathes

_____ 10. <u>Either</u> of my brothers _____ me with my math.
  **A** helps
  **B** help

_____ 11. <u>Many</u> of the candles _____ burned down.
  **A** has
  **B** have

_____ 12. <u>Each</u> of our soccer players _____ wearing green shorts.
  **A** are
  **B** is

_____ 13. <u>One</u> of those stamps _____ worth a fortune.
  **A** is
  **B** are

_____ 14. <u>Either</u> of the two plans _____ workable.
  **A** is
  **B** are

_____ 15. <u>Everybody</u> within twenty miles _____ farm work.
  **A** do
  **B** does

# CHAPTER 26 Subject and Verb Agreement Review

**EXERCISE** Write the letter of the word or group of words that belongs in each underlined space.

Tonight is our end-of-the-year concert. Everybody in the band **(1)** _____ arrived on time. Each of us **(2)** _____ taken his or her spot, and we **(3)** _____ about to begin. I **(4)** _____ playing the saxophone for years, but I'm nervous because I **(5)** _____ ever played a solo before tonight. Sitting in the audience **(6)** _____ my mom, dad, and younger brother. My family never **(7)** _____ one of my concerts.

It **(8)** _____ almost time to begin. Both Terry and Jamal **(9)** _____, "Don't worry. You'll do great!" The curtain is rising, and the audience **(10)** _____ getting quiet. Wish me luck!

_____ 1. **A** has
       **B** have
       **C** having
       **D** have had

_____ 2. **A** has
       **B** have
       **C** having
       **D** have had

_____ 3. **A** be
       **B** were
       **C** is
       **D** are

_____ 4. **A** has
       **B** been
       **C** has been
       **D** have been

_____ 5. **A** does
       **B** doesn't
       **C** haven't
       **D** hasn't

_____ 6. **A** am
       **B** is
       **C** was
       **D** are

_____ 7. **A** miss
       **B** misses
       **C** missing
       **D** have missed

_____ 8. **A** be
       **B** is
       **C** were
       **D** are

_____ 9. **A** has whispered
       **B** whispering
       **C** whisper
       **D** whispers

_____ 10. **A** were
       **B** are
       **C** is
       **D** am

Name _____ Date _____

# CHAPTER 27  Comparison of Adjectives and Adverbs

**[27A]** Most adjectives and adverbs have three degrees of comparison: the positive, the comparative, and the superlative.

> **EXERCISE** Circle the correct adjective or adverb and label it P for positive, C for comparative, or S for superlative.

_____ 1. This is the (longer, longest) of the two books.

_____ 2. Of my three brothers, Kevin is the (taller, tallest).

_____ 3. Which day was the (colder, coldest), Monday, Thursday, or Friday?

_____ 4. Which can run (fast, faster), the cheetah or the impala?

_____ 5. This box is (light, lighter).

_____ 6. Kim reads (quickly, more quickly).

_____ 7. In class no one works (harder, more harder) than Clarence.

_____ 8. This crate is (heavier, heaviest) than that one.

_____ 9. Denny writes (quickly, more quickly) than Dilbert.

_____ 10. Brandon is the (stronger, strongest) boy in our class.

_____ 11. Of all the clerks, Angie works the (more efficiently, most efficiently).

_____ 12. Kayla is (smart, smarter).

_____ 13. Today was the (hotter, hottest) day of the year.

_____ 14. The cat was (near, nearer) the fireplace.

_____ 15. That was the (narrow, narrowest) crack I have ever seen.

_____ 16. It would be hard for Nell to be (happier, happiest) than Danielle today.

_____ 17. Ken is (helpless, more helpless) at the computer.

_____ 18. We walked to the store (slowly, most slowly).

_____ 19. Friar Tuck was very (merry, merrily).

_____ 20. Mary wasn't sure which was (easier, easiest), running or walking.

_____ 21. Paul is the (taller, tallest) member of the basketball team.

_____ 22. Does the horse or the donkey run (faster, fastest)?

# CHAPTER 27  Degree of Comparison

**[27A.1]** Add *-er* to form the comparative degree and *–est* to form the superlative degree of one-syllable modifiers.

**[27A.2]** Use *-er* or the word *more* to form the comparative degree and *-est* or the word *most* to form the superlative degree of two-syllable modifiers.

**[27A.3]** Use *more* to form the comparative degree and *most* to form the superlative degree of modifiers with three or more syllables.

**EXERCISE** Choose the correct adjective or adverb for each sentence.

_____ 1. Of all the ski slopes, this is the _____ one.
  A  steeper
  B  steepest

_____ 2. Jane's ten-speed bike is the _____ in town.
  A  newer
  B  newest

_____ 3. Which of those two jackknives is the _____ one?
  A  sharper
  B  sharpest

_____ 4. Which is the _____ lawn in the neighborhood?
  A  greener
  B  greenest

_____ 5. Whose uniform is _____, Jerry's or mine?
  A  cleaner
  B  cleanest

_____ 6. Of the ten books I've read this year, *Light in the Forest* was the _____.
  A  more enjoyable
  B  most enjoyable

_____ 7. Of the five piano players, Barry performs the _____.
  A  more skillfully
  B  most skillfully

_____ 8. My sister folds clothes _____ than I do.
  A  more rapidly
  B  most rapidly

_____ 9. The girl played _____ than the boy.
  A  more merrily
  B  most merrily

_____ 10. Anna is _____ than my sister.
  A  more talkative
  B  most talkative

_____ 11. I was _____ in my bed than on the floor.
  A  more comfortable
  B  most comfortable

_____ 12. Of all the actors, my sister played her role _____.
  A  more happily
  B  most happily

_____ 13. This compact disc player is _____ than that one.
  A  more automated
  B  most automated

_____ 14. Jake is _____ than Harry.
  A  more athletic
  B  most athletic

# CHAPTER 27  Degree of Comparison

**EXERCISE** Write the correct modifier for each sentence on the line provided.

1. Which is (nearer, nearest), Chicago or Detroit?
2. Which city has the (taller, tallest) building in the United States?
3. Which is the (cooler, coolest) city today, Chicago, Denver, or Houston?
4. Which planet rotates (faster, fastest), Mercury or Venus?
5. Which planet is (brighter, brightest), Venus, Mars, or Jupiter?
6. Jupiter is bright, but Venus is (brighter, more bright).
7. Which of your two telescopes is (more powerful, most powerful)?
8. Asian elephants are (smaller, more small) than African elephants.
9. There are (fewer, more few) elephants in Asia than Africa.
10. An alligator mother guards her eggs (carefuller, more carefully) than a turtle mother does.
11. An antelope changes direction (quicklier, more quickly) than a cheetah.
12. Chimpanzees are (dangerouser, more dangerous) than gorillas.
13. Peacocks seem (colorfuller, more colorful) in the sun than in the shade.
14. The goldfish is (more visible, most visible) than the snail in the aquarium.
15. The dolphin is one of the (smarter, smartest) mammals.
16. Which ocean is (lower, lowest), the Atlantic or the Pacific?
17. Yosemite Falls is (higher, more high) than Niagara Falls.
18. Ed thinks the mountains are (more beautiful, most beautiful) than the ocean.
19. However, I find the seashore (enjoyabler, more enjoyable) than the mountains.

# CHAPTER 27  Irregular Comparison

**EXERCISE** Circle the correct adjective or adverb for each sentence.

1. Dogs spend (much, more, most) time at play.

2. Dogs spend the (many, more, most) time sleeping.

3. The weather is the (bad, worse, worst) in January.

4. Jim has picked even (many, more, most) blueberries than Joe.

5. Sheila, however, has picked the (many, more, most) of all.

6. The explorers had very (little, less, least) meat left.

7. They had (little, less, least) bread than meat.

8. (Little, Less, Least) of all was their supply of dry fruit.

9. In the first set, Norma played very (well, better, best).

10. In the second set, she played even (well, best, better).

11. In the final set, she played the (well, best, better).

12. Don's digital camera is quite (worst, good, best).

13. Marie's is (good, better, best) than Don's.

14. However, Dave's is the (better, best, good) I've seen.

15. Which do you like (better, best, good), animal stories or science fiction stories?

16. That song was the (bad, worse, worst) I've heard all year!

17. Of all the magician's tricks, I think the first one was (good, better, best).

# CHAPTER 27 — *Other* and *Else*

**[27B]** Watch for problems when comparing with the words *other* and *else*; avoid double comparisons and double negatives; and take care when using *good* and *well*.

**[27B.1]** Add *other* or *else* when comparing a member of a group to the rest of the group.

**EXERCISE** Write C if a sentence is correct or I if it is incorrect.

_____ 1. Chandra practiced the march longer than any member of the band.

_____ 2. Wendy runs faster than any other girl in the seventh grade.

_____ 3. Our dance was better than any other dance this year.

_____ 4. John throws harder than anyone else in my class.

_____ 5. Mr. Kim teaches better than any teacher at our school.

_____ 6. Michael donated more hours of service to the food bank than anyone else from my class.

_____ 7. Nan painted more pictures for the art show than anyone did.

_____ 8. Mr. Hooks coughed worse than anyone in class.

_____ 9. Sam got the assignment because he is smarter than any other student in the class.

_____ 10. My sister Delia sings more than anyone in my family.

_____ 11. Paul jumps higher than any kid on my street.

_____ 12. Martha harmonizes better than anyone else in the choir.

_____ 13. Stephanie writes more neatly than any other girl in English class.

_____ 14. Ivan played louder than any other drummer.

_____ 15. Tina wrote more poetry last year than anyone.

_____ 16. Maxine collected more bottle tops than anyone else at school.

_____ 17. Harold, the quarterback, threw harder than any football player at the game.

_____ 18. Steve swam faster than any boy at the meet.

_____ 19. Angela was more upset than the other girls.

_____ 20. Jermaine is more fun than any other person on the team.

_____ 21. No one else was as quiet as Sissy.

_____ 22. Shamika had more butterflies than anyone in the garden club.

_____ 23. Tammy ate more cookies than anyone else did.

# CHAPTER 27  Double Comparisons and Double Negatives

**[27B.2]** Do not use both *-er* and *more* to form the comparative degree or both *-est* and *most* to form the superlative degree.

**EXERCISE** Choose the correct word(s) to complete each sentence.

____ 1. We haven't had ____ to eat since morning.
  A  nothing
  B  anything

____ 2. My cat is ____ than yours.
  A  bigger
  B  more bigger

____ 3. Hob hasn't practiced ____ of his exercises yet.
  A  any
  B  none

____ 4. I'm not going to wear ____ tie tonight.
  A  no
  B  any

____ 5. Ruth worked on her project ____ than Ben.
  A  slowly
  B  more slowly

____ 6. That film started ____ than the other one.
  A  later
  B  more later

____ 7. Stuart claims he didn't tell ____ our secret.
  A  anyone
  B  no one

____ 8. Chen answered the questions ____ of all.
  A  eagerliest
  B  most eagerly

____ 9. A little glass of pineapple juice wouldn't hurt ____.
  A  anyone
  B  no one

____ 10. Sophie doesn't know ____ about this movie.
  A  anything
  B  nothing

____ 11. I could ____ leave town without a spare tire in the car.
  A  ever
  B  never

____ 12. My dog is ____ than yours.
  A  wetter
  B  more wetter

____ 13. Rose's story was the ____ of any student's story.
  A  shortest
  B  most shortest

____ 14. My dog would ____ bite you.
  A  ever
  B  never

____ 15. Don't you have ____ games this weekend?
  A  no
  B  any

____ 16. Aren't you taking ____ to the party?
  A  something
  B  nothing

____ 17. Suzanne's house is ____ than yours.
  A  closer
  B  more closer

____ 18. Eleanor said she wouldn't ____ mow a wet lawn again.
  A  ever
  B  never

Name _____ Date _____

# CHAPTER 27  Double Comparisons and Double Negatives

**EXERCISE** Write the correct word(s) to complete each sentence.

_____ 1. Everyone finished the assignment (quicklier, more quickly) than I did.

_____ 2. When the awards were handed out, I didn't get (none, any).

_____ 3. There aren't (any, no) snapping turtles in this lake.

_____ 4. Yesterday was the (rainiest, most rainiest) day all week.

_____ 5. Jerri didn't see (anyone, no one) familiar at the dance.

_____ 6. Ken jumped (farther, more farther) than anyone else on the track team.

_____ 7. The sunset was the (prettiest, most prettiest) I had ever seen.

_____ 8. Lemons smell (fresher, more fresh) than oranges.

_____ 9. I haven't done (any, none) of my homework yet.

_____ 10. The baking chocolate was (bitter, more bitter) than regular chocolate.

_____ 11. My mom drives the (smallest, most smallest) car I have ever seen.

_____ 12. Haven't you (ever, never) seen that picture before?

_____ 13. Some of the (specialist, most special) moments came at the end of the show.

_____ 14. I can swim (faster, more faster) than Robin.

_____ 15. Winter in Alaska is (colder, more colder) than it is in Arizona.

_____ 16. Dad can't (ever, never) find his glasses.

_____ 17. Mom and Dad don't have (no, any) objections to our plans for the barbecue.

_____ 18. Mom arrived at the play (later, more later) than she had expected.

Name _____   Date _____

## CHAPTER 27  *Good* or *Well*?

**Good** is always an adjective. **Well** is usually an adverb. However, when the word *well* means "in good health," it is used as an adjective.

**EXERCISE** Write either *good* or *well* to correctly complete each sentence.

1. This pen writes _____.

2. The music sounds _____.

3. His haircut looks _____.

4. The concert was _____.

5. Do the bells sound _____?

6. Alex's pitch was _____.

7. Sue is feeling _____.

8. That coat feels _____.

9. Yesterday's weather was _____ enough for a picnic.

10. Make sure you wash the dishes _____.

11. This engine purrs along very _____.

12. With flippers on, Dan swims pretty _____.

13. We all had a _____ time at the zoo.

14. Phil did very _____ on his math test.

15. This silk feels _____ on my skin.

16. I can't see very _____ without my glasses.

17. Kim can solve math problems as _____ as a computer can.

18. The mechanics checked the engine to be sure it ran _____.

19. The flowers in your bouquet smell _____.

Name _____  Date _____

# CHAPTER 27  Using Adjectives and Adverbs Review

**EXERCISE** Read the passage and write the letter of the modifier that belongs in each underlined space.

Ingrid is my **(1)** _____ friend. She is one of the **(2)** _____ people I know. One of her **(3)** _____ games is chess. She plays better than **(4)** _____ at school. It's amazing how much **(5)** _____ she plans her moves than **(6)** _____ player. We all had a **(7)** _____ time watching her win yesterday's tournament. Her competitors didn't have **(8)** _____ chance of winning! In the future I would like to spend **(9)** _____ time playing chess. Someday I hope to play the game as **(10)** _____ as Ingrid does.

_____ 1. **A** best
  **B** better
  **C** more better
  **D** bestest

_____ 2. **A** nicer
  **B** nicest
  **C** more nice
  **D** most nice

_____ 3. **A** favorite
  **B** more favorite
  **C** most favorite
  **D** favoritest

_____ 4. **A** anyone
  **B** anyone other
  **C** anyone ever
  **D** anyone else

_____ 5. **A** quicklier
  **B** quickliest
  **C** more quickly
  **D** more quick

_____ 6. **A** any
  **B** any other
  **C** no other
  **D** another

_____ 7. **A** better
  **B** well
  **C** good
  **D** best

_____ 8. **A** nothing
  **B** none
  **C** any
  **D** no

_____ 9. **A** more
  **B** much
  **C** most
  **D** many

_____ 10. **A** better
  **B** best
  **C** good
  **D** well

# CHAPTER 28 — First Words and the Pronoun *I*

**[28A.1]** Capitalize the first word in a sentence.
**[28.A.5]** Capitalize the pronoun *I*, both alone and in contractions.

**EXERCISE** Write correctly each word that should be capitalized.

1. yesterday's rain helped our garden.
2. did you see what i just did?
3. next year i'd like a part-time job.
4. i love that new song.
5. a sculpture was standing in front of the school.
6. my sister is president of the student body.
7. elaine registered for social studies, but i don't think i'm going to.
8. the boys like to play baseball, but i don't.
9. our car is very old.
10. before i wash the car, would you vacuum it?
11. my class went to the airport yesterday.
12. that's when i saw my first helicopter.
13. i'd seen helicopters in movies and on television.
14. i just hadn't ever been close to one before.
15. no other aircraft can stand still in the air and go straight up and down.
16. i think i'll get a pilot's license when i get older.
17. cats are interesting animals.
18. they have incredible balance.

# CHAPTER 28  Proper Nouns

**[28A.6]** Capitalize proper nouns and their abbreviations.

**EXERCISE** Select the answer that shows all the words that should be capitalized in each sentence.

_____ 1. Is mono lake on the california border?
  A  Mono, California
  B  Lake, California
  C  Mono, Lake, California
  D  Mono, Lake, California, Border

_____ 2. In 1901, king gillette of chicago patented the first safety razor.
  A  King, Gillette
  B  Gillette, Chicago
  C  Chicago
  D  King, Gillette, Chicago

_____ 3. The dog snoopy was drawn by charles schulz.
  A  Charles, Schulz
  B  Snoopy, Charles, Schulz
  C  Dog, Snoopy
  D  Dog, Snoopy, Schulz

_____ 4. During winter people from detroit visit the south.
  A  Winter, Detroit, South
  B  Detroit, South
  C  Detroit, People
  D  Detroit, Winter, South, People

_____ 5. Turn south on third avenue and drive along the east river.
  A  Third, River
  B  Third, Avenue, East
  C  Third, Avenue, East, River
  D  East River

_____ 6. The people of haiti won their independence from france in 1804.
  A  Haiti, Independence
  B  France, Independence
  C  Haiti, France
  D  Haiti, France, People

_____ 7. In 1985 and 1986, halley's comet approached the earth.
  A  Earth
  B  Halley's, Comet
  C  Halley's, Earth
  D  Halley's, Comet, Earth

_____ 8. At one time lassie was a famous dog in hollywood.
  A  Lassie, Hollywood
  B  Lassie, Dog, Hollywood
  C  Lassie
  D  Hollywood

_____ 9. The florida keys are southwest of miami.
  A  Florida, Keys
  B  Florida, Miami
  C  Florida, Keys, Miami
  D  Florida

_____ 10. In 1912, albert berry parachuted over st. louis.
  A  Albert Berry
  B  Albert Berry, St.
  C  Albert, Berry, St., Louis
  D  Albert, Berry, Parachuted, St., Louis

| Name | Date |

## CHAPTER 28 — Proper Nouns

**EXERCISE** Rewrite each paragraph correctly on the lines provided.

### Paragraph 1

In 1909, louis bleriot flew over the english channel. During world war I, he built aircraft for france. In 1927, he greeted lindbergh when lindbergh landed in france after flying solo across the atlantic ocean.

### Paragraph 2

Our cousins from sweden, ingmar and ingrid, plan to visit new york city. Part of new york city is the island of manhattan. ingmar and ingrid want to take a cruise around the island. Cruise boats shove off from the hudson river, which flows into the atlantic ocean. Our cousins also want to see rockefeller center, central park, and the empire state building.

# CHAPTER 28 Proper Adjectives

**[28 B.1]** Capitalize proper adjectives.

**EXERCISE** Select the proper adjective that should be capitalized in each sentence.

_____ 1. The tango, an argentine dance, became popular in 1910.
  A Tango
  B Argentine
  C Dance
  D Popular

_____ 2. In 1920, american women received the right to vote.
  A Women
  B Right
  C Vote
  D American

_____ 3. In 1928, the scottish scientist Alexander Fleming discovered penicillin.
  A Scientist
  B Penicillin
  C Scottish
  D Discovered

_____ 4. In the last century, many african nations gained their independence.
  A African
  B Century
  C Nations
  D Independence

_____ 5. Today many asian people live in Hawaii.
  A Asian
  B People
  C Live
  D Many

_____ 6. Have you ever tasted a spanish omelette?
  A Tasted
  B Spanish
  C Omelette
  D You

_____ 7. Some english gardens are very formal.
  A Gardens
  B Formal
  C Very
  D English

_____ 8. Supermarkets carry a variety of cheeses, including dutch cheese.
  A Variety
  B Cheese
  C Dutch
  D Carry

_____ 9. Our class learned that bubki is a tasty polish bread.
  A Bubki
  B Polish
  C Bread
  D Class

_____ 10. The city of San Diego is very near the mexican border.
  A Border
  B City
  C Near
  D Mexican

_____ 11. At the festival japanese dancers perform outside for everyone to watch.
  A Dancers
  B Perform
  C Japanese
  D Watch

_____ 12. We listened to a radio program featuring irish folk songs.
  A Irish
  B Folk songs
  C Radio
  D Program

# CHAPTER 28  Proper Adjectives

**EXERCISE** On the lines provided, write correctly the proper adjectives that should be capitalized in the following paragraphs.

Our ski resort was located near a swiss village. During our stay my brother and I learned some german words. We also learned to speak a bit of french and italian.

One evening the resort librarian invited a guest to tell us african folktales. On another night we listened to celtic legends. The last weekend we were there, a band played irish music while we danced in the ballroom. Later that same evening, we danced to beautiful spanish music on the international radio station.

Before we left, we took a bus to a nearby town, where we visited a museum that holds incredible european artifacts.

# CHAPTER 28 Titles

**[28 B.2]** Capitalize the titles of people and works of art.

> **EXERCISE** Write correctly the word that should be capitalized in each sentence. If the sentence is correct, write the words *no error* on the line.

1. The bill was introduced by senator Harkin from Iowa.
2. Is Olympia Snowe a senator from Maine?
3. One president with a military background was general Eisenhower.
4. The chair on the right of the stage is for you, governor.
5. Your appointment with dr. Garrison is at 2 P.M.
6. We received a newsletter from congresswoman Hayes.
7. Will you look at this back tooth, doctor?
8. The New Deal was the work of president Franklin D. Roosevelt.
9. Did you hear Chief Figaro speak on fire safety?
10. Please face the camera, judge.
11. The voters have re-elected mayor Barillos.
12. Frank saluted lieutenant Clarke on the parade ground.
13. We listened to ms. Franklin's speech on television.
14. Britain's prince William graduated from the University of St Andrews.
15. May I borrow your sweater, mom?
16. Did you write to your sister this week?
17. That jacket belongs to my dad.
18. This time, dad, I put all my money into my savings account.
19. Does your grandfather still work at the store?
20. I saw grandmother at the supermarket.
21. The funniest person in our family is aunt Ruth.
22. My uncle works in a lawyer's office.
23. Where did you put my umbrella, sis?

# CHAPTER 28 Titles of Works

**EXERCISE** Rewrite each sentence correctly on the line provided.

1. Have you read *History in review*?

2. My teacher assigned the chapter "The industrial revolution" for homework.

3. Did you read the article "The Future of capitalism"?

4. I like the song "Leaving for the promised Land."

5. The first full-length film, *the story of the Kelly Gang*, was shown in 1905.

6. Have you read Robert Frost's poem "The Road not Taken"?

7. Have you seen the painting, *Dancers practicing at the bar*?

8. Fred read the award-winning article in *USA today*.

9. Paula recited "the eagle" by Tennyson.

10. Rob played "The british grenadier" on his trombone.

11. "Alexander's ragtime band" was one of the first examples of jazz.

12. Did you read the article entitled "the first trip to Saturn"?

Name _____  Date _____

# CHAPTER 28 Capital Letters Review

**EXERCISE** Read the paragraph and decide which underlined words should be capitalized. Write the letter of the correct answer. If the underlined words contain no error, choose D.

Yesterday I told my **(1)** <u>cousin mary jane</u> about my family's vacation to **(2)** <u>Yellowstone national park</u>, which is located in **(3)** <u>Wyoming, Montana, and Idaho</u>. I told her how much I liked **(4)** <u>old faithful and fort yellowstone</u>. I also loved seeing all the animals—I was really hoping we'd see a grizzly bear! We didn't see any bears, but we did see some **(5)** <u>American bison and north American elk</u>. **(6)** <u>At a gift shop, mom bought a souvenir painting called "the buffalo of yellowstone."</u> I bought a book called **(7)** <u>"Old Faithful: Historic Highlights."</u> We stayed in a **(8)** <u>hotel in cody, wyoming</u>. **(9)** <u>One night in cody, we ate at a fantastic mexican restaurant</u>. It was a great vacation!

_____ 1. **A** cousin Mary jane
**B** cousin Mary Jane
**C** Cousin Mary Jane
**D** No error

_____ 2. **A** Yellowstone National Park
**B** Yellowstone National park
**C** yellowstone national park
**D** No error

_____ 3. **A** Wyoming, montana, and idaho
**B** wyoming, montana, and idaho
**C** Wyoming, Montana, and idaho
**D** No error

_____ 4. **A** Old Faithful and Fort yellowstone
**B** Old Faithful and Fort Yellowstone
**C** Old faithful and fort Yellowstone
**D** No error

_____ 5. **A** American Bison and north American Elk
**B** american bison and north american elk
**C** American bison and North American elk
**D** No error

_____ 6. **A** At a gift shop, Mom bought a souvenir painting called "The Buffalo of yellowstone."
**B** At a gift shop, mom bought a souvenir painting called "The buffalo of Yellowstone."
**C** At a gift shop, Mom bought a souvenir painting called "The Buffalo of Yellowstone."
**D** No error

_____ 7. **A** Old Faithful: historic highlights
**B** Old faithful: historic highlights
**C** Old faithful: Historic highlights
**D** No error

_____ 8. **A** hotel in Cody, Wyoming
**B** Hotel in Cody, Wyoming
**C** hotel in cody, Wyoming
**D** No error

_____ 9. **A** One night in Cody, we ate at a fantastic mexican restaurant.
**B** One night in cody, we ate at a fantastic Mexican restaurant.
**C** One night in Cody, we ate at a fantastic Mexican restaurant.
**D** No error

# CHAPTER 29  End Marks

**[29 A.1]** Place a **period** after a statement, after an opinion, and after a command or a request made in a normal tone of voice.
**[29 A.2]** Place a **question mark** after a sentence that asks a question.
**[29 A.3]** Place an **exclamation point** after a sentence that states strong feeling, after a command or request that expresses great excitement, and after an interjection.

> **EXERCISE** Decide whether each sentence should end with a period, a question mark, or an exclamation point.

_____ 1. Keep your eye on the third baseman
  A period
  B question mark
  C exclamation point

_____ 2. Did you go to the softball game
  A period
  B question mark
  C exclamation point

_____ 3. What an exciting game this is
  A period
  B question mark
  C exclamation point

_____ 4. The umpire called him out
  A period
  B question mark
  C exclamation point

_____ 5. Take a seat in the bleachers next to Ron
  A period
  B question mark
  C exclamation point

_____ 6. Our team is leading the league so far this season
  A period
  B question mark
  C exclamation point

_____ 7. Will you try out for the team next year
  A period
  B question mark
  C exclamation point

_____ 8. Do you have a mitt of your own
  A period
  B question mark
  C exclamation point

_____ 9. Will that player steal second base
  A period
  B question mark
  C exclamation point

_____ 10. Is that two home runs in a row
  A period
  B question mark
  C exclamation point

_____ 11. Boy, the other team sure is rattled
  A period
  B question mark
  C exclamation point

_____ 12. Stop that grounder, Wes
  A period
  B question mark
  C exclamation point

# CHAPTER 29 End Marks

**EXERCISE** Read each sentence and then write the correct end mark.

1. Dogs make the best pets
2. Is that your dog
3. I own a cocker spaniel
4. Did you see the size of that Great Dane
5. Watch out
6. Close the gate before that dog escapes
7. Today is a terrific day for a picnic
8. Should we go to Kenney Park or Rosewood Park
9. Call Jan and Peter and invite them
10. Pack two kinds of sandwiches
11. I like pickles on my sandwich
12. I'll make some lemonade
13. Should we take some potato salad too
14. What's splashing against the windows
15. The forecast mentioned occasional showers
16. Boy, this is some shower
17. We'll take a rain check on the picnic
18. What exactly is a rain check
19. Hurry and shut the door
20. Let's just eat inside

# CHAPTER 29  Periods with Abbreviations

**[29 A.4]** Use a period with most abbreviations.

**EXERCISE** Write correctly the abbreviation in each sentence.

_____ 1. Wall St is the financial center of New York.

_____ 2. Do you know the location of St Lawrence University?

_____ 3. At exactly 7:30 AM, my alarm rang.

_____ 4. Dr DeBakey performed many heart operations.

_____ 5. The Marshall Plan was named after Gen George Marshall.

_____ 6. This year Labor Day falls on Mon, September 6.

_____ 7. The school year began on Sept 9.

_____ 8. In 332 BC, Alexander the Great conquered Egypt.

_____ 9. At birth a baby giraffe is 6 ft tall.

_____ 10. The Peace Corps was founded by Pres John Kennedy.

_____ 11. The tennis shoes weighed more than 1 lb each!

_____ 12. Ms Susan MacIllwain ran for club vice president.

_____ 13. One of Mr George Orwell's best-known books is _1984_.

_____ 14. My room is 9 yds long.

_____ 15. I lived on Peach Ave when I went to middle school.

_____ 16. Lt Baines is in the Air Force.

_____ 17. My brother, Josh Stephens Jr, is a football player.

_____ 18. She added 1 tsp of salt to the flour.

_____ 19. We went on a cruise led by Capt John Malgoza.

_____ 20. We went to my grandparents' house every Sun when I was young.

_____ 21. In AD 1492, the Spanish defeated the last of the Moors.

Name _____  Date _____

## CHAPTER 29 — Commas with a Series

**[29 B.1]** Use commas to separate items in a series.

**EXERCISE** Choose the sentence that is punctuated correctly.

_____ 1. Snakes turtles and frogs all hibernate.
   A  Snakes, turtles and frogs all hibernate.
   B  Snakes turtles, and frogs all hibernate.
   C  Snakes, turtles, and frogs all hibernate.

_____ 2. Jackie put meat bread beans and fruit in the shopping cart.
   A  Jackie put meat, bread, beans, and fruit in the shopping cart.
   B  Jackie put, meat, bread, beans and fruit in the shopping cart.
   C  Jackie put meat bread, beans and, fruit in the shopping cart.

_____ 3. Luke ate breakfast brushed his teeth and got dressed before school.
   A  Luke ate breakfast, brushed his teeth and got dressed before school.
   B  Luke ate breakfast, brushed his teeth, and got dressed before school.
   C  Luke ate breakfast, brushed, his teeth, and got dressed, before school.

_____ 4. Little kids often like to play with pots pans and wooden spoons.
   A  Little kids often like to play, with pots, pans and wooden spoons.
   B  Little kids often like to play with pots, pans, and wooden spoons.
   C  Little kids often like to play with pots, pans and wooden spoons.

_____ 5. Apes are known for their intelligence playfulness and acrobatic stunts.
   A  Apes are known, for their intelligence, playfulness, and acrobatic stunts.
   B  Apes are known for their, intelligence, playfulness, and acrobatic stunts.
   C  Apes are known for their intelligence, playfulness, and acrobatic stunts.

_____ 6. Today I have to go to the dentist return a shirt to the store and pick up the dry cleaning.
   A  Today, I have to go to the dentist, return a shirt, to the store, and pick up the dry cleaning.
   B  Today, I have to go, to the dentist, return a shirt, to the store, and pick up the dry cleaning.
   C  Today I have to go to the dentist, return a shirt to the store, and pick up the dry cleaning.

_____ 7. On the big day the wedding planner picked up the bride's bouquet got more table napkins and thanked the chef.
   A  On the big day, the wedding planner picked up the bride's bouquet, got more table napkins, and thanked the chef.
   B  On the big day, the wedding planner picked up, the bride's bouquet, got more table napkins, and thanked the chef.
   C  On the big day the wedding planner, picked up the bride's bouquet, got more table napkins and thanked the chef.

Name _____    Date _____

# CHAPTER 29 — Commas with a Series

**EXERCISE** Rewrite each sentence, adding commas where needed.

1. We have seen apes at the zoo on TV and in the movies.

2. Funny playful and friendly apes are favorites at the zoo.

3. Gorillas chimpanzees orangutans and gibbons are all apes.

4. Gorillas travel in packs walk on all fours and sometimes stand upright.

5. Gorillas in captivity drum on dishes trays and barrels.

6. Chimpanzees eat fruit birds and small animals.

7. Trained chimps ride bikes use tools and stand on their heads.

8. Orangutans are friendly childlike and stubborn.

9. Gibbons leap swing and run in trees.

10. The gibbon's voice is loud high-pitched and sharp.

Name _____ Date _____

## CHAPTER 29 — Adjectives Before a Noun

**[29 B.2]** Use a comma to separate two adjectives that precede a noun and that would read well with the word *and* between them.

> **EXERCISE** Rewrite the underlined words in each sentence, adding commas where needed. If the underlined section is correct as written, write the words *no error* on the line.

_____ 1. The <u>small weak kitten</u> was a newborn.

_____ 2. Joe's <u>short and humorous story</u> was about his vacation.

_____ 3. The <u>large colorful rug</u> came from China.

_____ 4. The <u>old heavy trunk</u> was in the attic.

_____ 5. Ruth is the <u>fastest most ambitious person</u> on the track team.

_____ 6. Several <u>faster stronger students</u> have tried to beat her records.

_____ 7. <u>Ten unruly children</u> waited in front of the library.

_____ 8. The <u>slow noisy traffic</u> is typical for a Friday.

_____ 9. It was a <u>hot dusty walk</u>.

_____ 10. All you will need is your <u>light green jacket</u>.

_____ 11. Becky wants to visit the <u>shrinking Amazon rainforest</u>.

_____ 12. A <u>strong southerly wind</u> brought rain to our fields.

# CHAPTER 29 Compound Sentences

**[29 B.3]** Use a comma before a coordinating conjunction that joins the parts of a compound sentence.

**EXERCISE** Choose the sentence that is punctuated correctly. If the sentence is correct as written, choose *No error*.

_____ 1. In the United States Mother's Day is in May and Father's Day is in June.
   A   In the United States, Mother's Day is in May, and Father's Day is in June.
   B   In the United States Mother's Day is in May and, Father's Day is in June.
   C   No error

_____ 2. In Los Angeles many people drive cars but in New York City many people use the subways.
   A   In Los Angeles many people drive cars, but in New York City many people use the subways.
   B   In Los Angeles, many people drive cars but in New York City, many people use the subways.
   C   No error

_____ 3. The Colosseum is a famous ruin and thousands of tourists in Rome visit it every day.
   A   The Colosseum is a famous ruin and thousands of tourists in Rome, visit it every day.
   B   The Colosseum is a famous ruin, and thousands of tourists in Rome visit it every day.
   C   No error

_____ 4. Today tourists can visit parts of the Colosseum and imagine it with 45,000 spectators.
   A   Today, tourists can visit parts, of the Colosseum and imagine it with 45,000 spectators.
   B   Today tourists can visit parts of the Colosseum, and imagine it with 45,000 spectators.
   C   No error

_____ 5. There have been many gold rushes, but, few people strike it rich.
   A   There have been many gold rushes, but few people strike it rich.
   B   There have been many, gold rushes but few people, strike it rich.
   C   No error

_____ 6. The audience became silent and the pianist began to play.
   A   The audience became silent and the pianist, began to play.
   B   The audience became silent, and the pianist began to play.
   C   No error

_____ 7. My sister just turned sixteen and she wants to get her driver's license.
   A   My sister just turned sixteen, and she wants to get her driver's license.
   B   My sister, just turned sixteen and, she wants to get her driver's license.
   C   No error

# CHAPTER 29 Compound Sentences

**EXERCISE** Write C if a sentence is correctly punctuated or I if it is incorrect.

(1) The ancient Egyptians made paper and some of it still exists. (2) They gathered papyrus plants and shaped the stems into scrolls. (3) Papyrus did not grow everywhere but other materials could also be used. (4) Some papermakers used rags and others used animal hides.

(5) In China, people first wrote on silk, but then someone invented paper. (6) The inventor gathered bark and rags and made a pulp. (7) He dried the mixture over a frame and the result was paper. (8) After that, the Chinese began making paper but no one else knew the formula. (9) In 751, Arabs captured some Chinese workmen and learned the secret. (10) Eventually a paper mill opened in Spain and the art of making paper spread.

(11) Today paper is not strong and in time it will decay. (12) Modern paper is made from wood and wood contains acids. (13) The acid is released slowly and eats the paper. (14) Records are kept on paper but the paper breaks down in 30 to 50 years. (15) These records must be reprinted or stored on microfilm.

1. \_\_\_\_
2. \_\_\_\_
3. \_\_\_\_
4. \_\_\_\_
5. \_\_\_\_
6. \_\_\_\_
7. \_\_\_\_
8. \_\_\_\_
9. \_\_\_\_
10. \_\_\_\_
11. \_\_\_\_
12. \_\_\_\_
13. \_\_\_\_
14. \_\_\_\_
15. \_\_\_\_

Name _____ Date _____

## CHAPTER 29 — Introductory Elements

**[29 B.4]** Use a comma after certain introductory words, phrases, or clauses.

> **EXERCISE** Choose the sentence that is punctuated correctly. If the sentence is already punctuated correctly, choose *No error*.

_____ 1. Yes prairie dogs are a kind of ground squirrel.
   A  Yes, prairie dogs are a kind of ground squirrel.
   B  Yes prairie dogs, are a kind of ground squirrel.
   C  No error

_____ 2. Against the evening sky the city skyline stood out clearly.
   A  Against the evening, sky the city skyline stood out clearly.
   B  Against the evening sky, the city skyline stood out clearly.
   C  No error

_____ 3. Why that must be your uncle at the door.
   A  Why, that must be your uncle at the door.
   B  Why that must be, your uncle at the door.
   C  No error

_____ 4. Well, I certainly didn't know that.
   A  Well I certainly, didn't know that.
   B  Well I certainly didn't know that.
   C  No error

_____ 5. During the break in the football game the band marched onto the field.
   A  During the break in the football game, the band marched onto the field.
   B  During the break, in the football game the band marched onto the field.
   C  No error

_____ 6. Sure tell me what really happened.
   A  Sure tell me, what really happened.
   B  Sure, tell me what really happened.
   C  No error

_____ 7. From the observation deck we watched the planes land.
   A  From the observation deck, we watched the planes land.
   B  From the observation, deck we watched the planes land.
   C  No error

_____ 8. No the koala is not really a bear.
   A  No the koala, is not really a bear.
   B  No, the koala is not really a bear.
   C  No error

_____ 9. At breakfast Sam ate a bowl of cereal with banana slices.
   A  At breakfast Sam, ate a bowl of cereal with banana slices.
   B  At breakfast Sam ate a bowl, of cereal, with banana slices.
   C  No error

_____ 10. From one generation to another folk songs are passed along.
   A  From one generation, to another folk songs are passed along.
   B  From one generation to another, folk songs are passed along.
   C  No error

# CHAPTER 29  Introductory Elements

**EXERCISE** Rewrite each sentence, adding a comma where needed.

1. In a pool or at the beach lifeguards are usually present.

2. Even with lifeguards present it is still a good idea to swim with a friend.

3. At the beach in rough water a swimmer could be knocked over.

4. Even on a nice day strong tides can be dangerous for all types of swimmers.

5. At a crowded waterfront you and a friend can watch over each other.

6. No don't float too far away on an inner tube.

7. Oh keep out of the way of that motorboat!

8. In shallow water near the shore most swimmers are safest.

# CHAPTER 29 Dates, Addresses, and Letters

**[29 B.5]** Use commas to separate elements in dates and addresses.
**[29 B.6]** Use a comma after the salutation of a friendly letter and after the closing of all letters.

**EXERCISE** Write A or B to indicate the item that is correctly written in each of the following pairs.

_____ 1. **A** 243 Elm Street Elgin IL
**B** 243 Elm Street, Elgin, IL

_____ 2. **A** Monday, April 1, 1985
**B** Monday April 1, 1985

_____ 3. **A** University Hospital Chapel Hill North Carolina
**B** University Hospital, Chapel Hill, North Carolina

_____ 4. **A** 89 Southard Avenue, Rockville Center, New York 11570
**B** 89 Southard Avenue Rockville Center New York, 11570

_____ 5. **A** February 20 1962
**B** February 20, 1962

_____ 6. **A** Dear Mom,
**B** Dear Mom

_____ 7. **A** Very truly yours
**B** Very truly yours,

_____ 8. **A** 47 Main Street Clearwater, FL 33515
**B** 47 Main Street, Clearwater, FL 33515

_____ 9. **A** Respectfully,
**B** Respectfully

_____ 10. **A** May 29, 1917
**B** May 29 1917

_____ 11. **A** 123 Sunny Lane Ashland Ohio 44805
**B** 123 Sunny Lane, Ashland, Ohio 44805

_____ 12. **A** Saturday, June 15, 1985
**B** Saturday June 15, 1985

_____ 13. **A** Daniel Davidson, Oakland Highway, Nashua, New Hampshire 03062
**B** Daniel Davidson Oakland Highway, Nashua New Hampshire 03062

_____ 14. **A** My dearest love,
**B** My dearest love

_____ 15. **A** July 20, 1969
**B** July 20 1969

_____ 16. **A** 476 Pioneer Drive, Lansing, Michigan 48910
**B** 476 Pioneer Drive, Lansing, Michigan, 48910

_____ 17. **A** As, Always,
**B** As always,

_____ 18 **A** Dear friends,
**B** Dear friends

_____ 19. **A** 40 Bloomingdale Street, Boise, Idaho 06103
**B** 40 Bloomingdale Street Boise, Idaho 06103

_____ 20. **A** 221B Baker Street London
**B** 221B Baker Street, London

Name _____  Date _____

# CHAPTER 29  Parenthetical Expressions

**[29 C.2]** Use commas to set off parenthetical expressions.

**EXERCISE A** Write C if a sentence is correctly punctuated or I if it is incorrect.

_____ 1. To tell the truth, this movie is pretty dull.

_____ 2. However rock bands are often smaller than dance bands.

_____ 3. In my opinion your haircut is perfect.

_____ 4. Moreover, you did a great job in the play last night.

_____ 5. The color yellow, for example is associated with joy and cheerfulness.

_____ 6. In fact, my brother hasn't missed a day of school since kindergarten.

**EXERCISE B** Choose the sentence that is punctuated correctly. If the sentence is already punctuated correctly, choose *No error.*

_____ 7. A pink jellyfish by the way has a strange shape.
   A  A pink jellyfish, by the way has a strange shape.
   B  A pink jellyfish, by the way, has a strange shape.
   C  No error

_____ 8. Palominos, however, always have white manes.
   A  Palominos however always have white manes.
   B  Palominos however, always have white manes.
   C  No error

_____ 9. For instance forsythia blooms in early spring.
   A  For instance, forsythia blooms in early spring.
   B  For instance, forsythia, blooms in early spring.
   C  No error

_____ 10. The female mosquito, I believe, does not really bite.
   A  The female, mosquito, I believe does not really bite.
   B  The female mosquito I believe, does not really bite.
   C  No error

_____ 11. Indians once packaged food, in pottery, I think.
   A  Indians once packaged food in pottery, I think.
   B  Indians once packaged, food in pottery, I think.
   C  No error

_____ 12. Orchids generally speaking grow in the tropics.
   A  Orchids, generally speaking grow in the tropics.
   B  Orchids, generally speaking, grow in the tropics.
   C  No error

# CHAPTER 29  Parenthetical Expressions

**EXERCISE** Rewrite each sentence, adding a comma or commas where needed.

1. Parts of the Painted Desert of course are yellow and red.

2. The cuckoo clock is my favorite I guess.

3. Nevertheless wild pigs still roam the woods in South Carolina.

4. Life on the frontier was lonely on the other hand.

5. Consequently palm trees grow mainly in tropical places.

6. The weather at any rate should remain sunny.

7. The moon after all is a satellite of Earth.

8. In my opinion roses are the most beautiful flowers.

9. We should still I hope make it to the movie on time.

# CHAPTER 29 Appositives and Nonessential Elements

**[29 C.3]** Use commas to set off most appositives and appositive phrases.

**EXERCISE** Write C if a sentence is correctly punctuated or I if it is incorrect.

_____ 1. Drew Barrymore the famous actor, also directs.

_____ 2. Thomas Jefferson, one of the signers of the Declaration of Independence, was a writer.

_____ 3. Rachel my very observant friend, found five dollars.

_____ 4. Ross is the person you want to see.

_____ 5. Mick showed me his present, a new DVD player.

_____ 6. Charlie asked Mrs. Hoffman our biology teacher, about dissecting.

_____ 7. Keith is the one who plays guitar the best.

_____ 8. Ron the bass player, joined the group last.

_____ 9. I like the puppy, chasing his tail.

_____ 10. The puppy that has the red collar is the most playful.

_____ 11. Mr. Simpson our principal, enjoys listening to the band.

_____ 12. That comic the one on the left made his living impersonating famous people.

Name _____ Date _____

# CHAPTER 29  Appositives and Nonessential Elements

**EXERCISE** Rewrite each sentence, adding or deleting comma(s) where needed. If no commas are needed, write *no error* on the line.

1. Alaska, the largest state was once owned by Russia.
   _____

2. Have you met Paula my sister, from Denver?
   _____

3. Golden retrievers once thought of only as family pets are used to help the blind.
   _____

4. That poem, composed by my sister, won first prize in the contest.
   _____

5. Lou, working, quickly finished long before the rest of us.
   _____

6. My oldest cousin, Darlene, is a nurse.
   _____

7. Mrs. Grant a quiet woman enjoys, photography.
   _____

8. The tape, which contained all the information, was erased.
   _____

9. The game, that my brother likes best, is on sale this week.
   _____

10. Rob the team captain, is also a good student.
    _____

11. Mr. Andropov, my new neighbor, is from Russia.
    _____

12. Rose Wills, whom I have known for years is moving to Arkansas.
    _____

# CHAPTER 29 — End Marks and Commas Review

**EXERCISE** Read the passage and write the letter of the correct way to write each set of underlined words. If the underlined words contain no error, choose D.

---

(1) September 30 2009

(2) Dear Aunt Marcy

I hope you are doing (3) well. Mom and Dad probably told you that we just got back from (4) Washington, DC. (5) During our visit to the Lincoln Memorial I fell down the stairs and broke my ankle. (6) What luck! At the hospital emergency room, (7) Dr Keith Macy a very nice man set the bone. Without a doubt he saved my vacation. (8) Within a day or two, I was able to visit (9) the Air and Space Museum the White House and the National Archives. (10) All in all, I got to see everything I wanted to and I went home, a happy tourist.

(11) Your nephew,

Owen

---

_____ 1. A September 30, 2009
      B September 30, 2009,
      C September 30 2009,
      D No error

_____ 2. A Dear Aunt Marcy!
      B Dear Aunt Marcy,
      C Dear Aunt Marcy.
      D No error

_____ 3. A well, Mom and Dad
      B well Mom and Dad
      C well? Mom and Dad
      D No error

_____ 4. A Washington, D.C.
      B Washington, D,C.
      C Washington., D.C,
      D No error

_____ 5. A During our visit, to the Lincoln Memorial, I fell down
      B During our visit to the Lincoln Memorial I fell down,
      C During our visit to the Lincoln Memorial, I fell down
      D No error

_____ 6. A What luck? At
      B What luck, At
      C What luck. At
      D No error

_____ 7. A Dr. Keith Macy, a very nice man, set the bone.
      B Dr. Keith Macy a very nice man, set the bone.
      C Dr Keith Macy, a very nice man, set the bone.
      D No error

_continued_

# Chapter 29: End Marks and Commas Review *continued*

_____ 8. **A** Within, a day or two, I was able
       **B** Within a day, or two I was able
       **C** Within a day or two I was able,
       **D** No error

_____ 9. **A** the Air and Space, Museum the White House, and the National Archives.
       **B** the Air and Space Museum the White House, and the National Archives.
       **C** the Air and Space Museum, the White House, and the National Archives.
       **D** No error

_____ 10. **A** All in all, I got to see everything I wanted to and I went home, a happy tourist.
        **B** All in all, I got to see everything I wanted to, and I went home a happy tourist.
        **C** All in all, I got to see everything, I wanted to, and I went home a happy tourist.
        **D** No error

_____ 11. **A** Your nephew.
        **B** Your nephew
        **C** Your, nephew,
        **D** No error

# CHAPTER 30 Italics (Underlining) and Quotation Marks with Titles

**[30A.2]** Italicize (underline) the titles of long written or musical works that are published as a single unit. Also italicize (underline) the titles of paintings and sculptures and the names of vehicles.

**[30B.1]** Use quotation marks to enclose the titles of chapters, articles, stories, one-act plays, short poems, and songs.

> **EXERCISE** Decide whether italics or quotation marks should be used to punctuate the title(s) in each sentence.

_____ 1. One TV series I watch regularly is Survivor.
  A  italics
  B  quotation marks

_____ 2. The one-act opera Amahl and the Night Visitors was written by Gian-Carlo Menotti.
  A  italics
  B  quotation marks

_____ 3. Do you ever read issues of National Geographic World?
  A  italics
  B  quotation marks

_____ 4. The nuclear-powered submarine Nautilus can remain underwater for months.
  A  italics
  B  quotation marks

_____ 5. Vincent van Gogh's most famous painting is The Starry Night.
  A  italics
  B  quotation marks

_____ 6. The Garden Party is a short story by Katherine Mansfield.
  A  italics
  B  quotation marks

_____ 7. My brother reads every issue of Popular Mechanics.
  A  italics
  B  quotation marks

_____ 8. The movie The Wizard of Oz is shown frequently on TV.
  A  italics
  B  quotation marks

_____ 9. Tin Can on a Shingle is a book about a ship.
  A  italics
  B  quotation marks

_____ 10. The Highwayman is Alfred Noyes' best-known poem.
  A  italics
  B  quotation marks

_____ 11. Love Me Tender is a song based on an old folk song, I believe.
  A  italics
  B  quotation marks

_____ 12. The Dream Fulfilled is a chapter in the book.
  A  italics
  B  quotation marks

_____ 13. The TV series Masterpiece Theater has won many awards.
  A  italics
  B  quotation marks

_____ 14. Listen to the song I Heard It Through the Grapevine.
  A  italics
  B  quotation marks

# CHAPTER 30 — Italics (Underlining) and Quotation Marks with Titles

> **EXERCISE** Correctly punctuate the title(s) in the following sentences with quotation marks or underlining (for italics).

1. This essay called "Native Shores" is fascinating.

2. <u>Old Possum's Book of Practical Cats</u> by T.S. Eliot is a book of poems about cats.

3. The movie <u>Harry Potter and the Half-Blood Prince</u> is now available on DVD.

4. The Boston Pops played the Beethoven symphony known as <u>Eroica</u>.

5. Who designed the sculpture <u>Prometheus</u> in Rockefeller Plaza?

6. Robert Frost's poem "Mending Wall" is my favorite.

7. President John F. Kennedy wrote the book <u>Profiles in Courage</u>.

8. Robert Fulton called his steamboat the <u>Clermont</u>.

9. The song "Guinevere" is from a musical.

10. I read the poem "Paul Revere's Ride" in speech class.

11. "The Buck in the Hills" is a short story about hunting.

12. <u>The Kiss</u> is a famous painting by Gustav Klimt.

13. Have you read the chapter "The Colonies Win Freedom"?

14. Our daily newspaper is the <u>Nashville Banner</u>.

15. The last episode of <u>M*A*S*H</u> aired in 1983.

16. The article "A Lost Son Is Found" was in a magazine.

## CHAPTER 30 Direct and Indirect Quotations

**[30B.2]** Use quotation marks to enclose a person's exact words.

**EXERCISE** Decide whether a direct or indirect quotation is included in each sentence.

_____ 1. "Are woodpeckers carpenters?" Henry asked.
   **A** direct quotation
   **B** indirect quotation

_____ 2. "Sure they are," Mac replied.
   **A** direct quotation
   **B** indirect quotation

_____ 3. He added that they drill holes in trees.
   **A** direct quotation
   **B** indirect quotation

_____ 4. "Are robins carpenters too?" asked Mary.
   **A** direct quotation
   **B** indirect quotation

_____ 5. Joe said, "No, robins are masons. They plaster the inside of their nests with mud."
   **A** direct quotation
   **B** indirect quotation

_____ 6. Shawna said, "A hummingbird must be an upholsterer, then."
   **A** direct quotation
   **B** indirect quotation

_____ 7. José asked her why she thought that.
   **A** direct quotation
   **B** indirect quotation

_____ 8. She replied that hummingbirds pad their nests with moss.
   **A** direct quotation
   **B** indirect quotation

_____ 9. "Orioles are master weavers," announced Antonio.
   **A** direct quotation
   **B** indirect quotation

_____ 10. He added, "They weave cradles from fibers of grass and bits of string."
   **A** direct quotation
   **B** indirect quotation

_____ 11. They all agreed that birds are skillful workers.
   **A** direct quotation
   **B** indirect quotation

_____ 12. "Why do you say that?" Tim asked.
   **A** direct quotation
   **B** indirect quotation

# CHAPTER 30  Capital Letters with Direct Quotations

**[30B.3]** Capitalize the first word of a direct quotation.

> **EXERCISE** Underline any additional words that need to be capitalized in the following dialogue.

1. "<u>many</u> people," Rita said, "<u>think</u> computers are smart."

2. "<u>not</u> me," Bill replied. "<u>they</u> really aren't at all."

3. "<u>even</u> the most complicated computer," Rita continued, "is no match for the human brain."

4. "<u>actually</u>," Bill said, "computers are helpless without humans."

5. "<u>that's</u> right," <u>rita</u> agreed. "<u>they</u> need someone to give them instructions."

6. Bill added, "<u>that's</u> what computer programmers do."

7. "<u>don't</u> you think that would be a lot of fun?" Rita asked.

8. "I'd like to learn programming," Bill said. "<u>then</u> I could give the instructions."

9. "<u>and</u> have the machine follow them," Rita added.

10. "<u>now</u> that would be exciting," Bill said.

11. Rita said, "<u>well</u>, let's learn."

12. "<u>my</u> older brother knows a lot about programming," Bill said.

13. "<u>he</u> could help get us started," Rita said, "and so could Ms. Rodriguez at school."

14. "<u>we</u> can get books from the library too," <u>bill</u> said. "<u>what</u> are we waiting for?"

Name _____  Date _____

**CHAPTER 30**  **Commas and End Marks with Direct Quotations**

**[30B.4]** Use a comma between a direct quotation and the speaker tag. Place the comma inside the closing quotation marks.

**[30B.5]** Put a period inside the closing quotation marks when the end of the quotation comes at the end of a sentence.

The same is true of question marks and exclamation marks that end a quotation.

**EXERCISE** Write C if the punctuation in each sentence is correct or I if it is incorrect. Revise any incorrect commas or quotation marks.

_____ 1. "Kites have been popular for thousands of years", Mrs. Carson said.

_____ 2. She added, "They are flown in all parts of the world."

_____ 3. "Aren't they especially popular in parts of Asia"? Maria asked.

_____ 4. "Koreans fly kites during the first days of the New Year", Mike said.

_____ 5. He added ", That's one way they used to celebrate."

_____ 6. "In Japan," Mrs. Carson said, "kites are flown as part of a festival in May."

_____ 7. Mike added, "In China there's a special day each year called Kite Day".

_____ 8. He said, "Thousands of kites are flown at these festivals."

_____ 9. "The kites are made in all shapes, colors, and sizes", Mrs. Carson said.

_____ 10. "Some are shaped like dragons" she said "and some look like fish."

_____ 11. "And some," Mike added, "are shaped liked butterflies and birds."

_____ 12. "What kind of kites will we make?" Maria asked.

# CHAPTER 30 — Writing Dialogue

**[30B.6]** When writing dialogue, begin a new paragraph each time the speaker changes.

**EXERCISE** Rewrite the following dialogue correctly on the lines below. Begin a new paragraph each time the speaker changes. Add or correct quotation marks and other punctuation as needed.

Pam asked, Do you want to come over to my house after school to finish your homework"? "That's a great idea, Bonnie answered, because we can also start talking about our social studies project." "When is the project due"? Pam asked. "We have to hand it in a week from this Friday", Bonnie answered. "That seems like a long ways off, Pam said, but it will be here before you know it." "That's true", Bonnie said, but we'll have the whole weekend to work on it, if we need it." "Maybe you can come over on Saturday, Pam said. "We can work for a while and then watch a movie." That sounds good to me, Bonnie said.

# CHAPTER 30 Italics and Quotation Marks Review

**EXERCISE** Write the letter of the correct answer for each underlined part in the following passage. If the underlined part contains no error, choose D.

One TV show I watch regularly is (1) the TV series "Lost". I also really like movies such as (2) "Star Wars: The Empire Strikes Back." My sister's current favorite movie is (3) *Pirates of the Caribbean: At World's End.* Dad is more of a magazine reader and especially likes (4) *National Geographic magazine.* Mom would rather read (5) classic novels like "Pride and Prejudice" than almost anything else.

The other night my mom (6) said "how will we ever agree on (7) which movie to watch tonight"?

(8) I suggested "we watch the new *Star Trek* movie."

(9) "My dad said, I'll watch anything with Bruce Willis."

(10) "How about if we watch a comedy"? my sister said. "We all like comedies."

Mom came up with a good solution. "The old Marx Brothers (11) movie *A Night at the Opera* is on TV tonight," she said.

My sister and I had never seen it. (12) We thought "it was hilarious."

_____ 1. **A** the TV series *Lost.*
**B** the TV series "Lost."
**C** the "TV series Lost".
**D** No error

_____ 2. **A** "Star Wars: The Empire Strikes Back."
**B** *Star Wars*: "The Empire Strikes Back".
**C** *Star Wars: The Empire Strikes Back.*
**D** No error

_____ 3. **A** "Pirates of the Caribbean: At World's End."
**B** "Pirates of the Caribbean: At World's End".
**C** "Pirates of the Caribbean:" At World's End.
**D** No error

_____ 4. **A** "National Geographic magazine."
**B** "National Geographic" magazine.
**C** *National Geographic* magazine.
**D** No error

_____ 5. **A** classic novels like *Pride and Prejudice*
**B** "classic novels like *Pride and Prejudice*"
**C** classic novels "like Pride and Prejudice"
**D** No error

_____ 6. **A** said, how will
**B** said "how will
**C** said, "How will
**D** No error

*continued*

# Chapter 30: Italics and Quotation Marks Review *continued*

_____ 7. **A** "which movie to watch tonight"?
      **B** which movie to watch tonight?"
      **C** which movie, "to watch tonight?"
      **D** No error

_____ 8. **A** I suggested we watch the new *Star Trek* movie.
      **B** I suggested, "We watch the new *Star Trek* movie."
      **C** I suggested we watch "the new *Star Trek* movie".
      **D** No error

_____ 9. **A** "My dad said I'll
      **B** My dad said, "I'll
      **C** My dad said, I'll
      **D** No error

_____ 10. **A** a comedy,"? my sister
       **B** a comedy?" my sister
       **C** a comedy? my sister
       **D** No error

_____ 11. **A** movie, "A Night at the Opera"
       **B** "movie A Night at the Opera"
       **C** movie "A Night at the Opera"
       **D** No error

_____ 12. **A** "We thought it was hilarious."
       **B** We thought it was hilarious.
       **C** We thought, It was hilarious.
       **D** No error

## CHAPTER 31  Apostrophes

**[31A]** The **apostrophe** (') is used to show ownership and to represent missing letters in contractions. It is also used with certain plurals.

**[31A.1]** Add 's to form the possessive of a singular noun.

**[31A.2]** Add only an apostrophe to form the possessive of a plural noun that ends in *s*.

**[31A.3]** Add 's to form the possessive of a plural noun that does not end in *s*.

---

**EXERCISE** Identify the underlined possessive noun as singular or plural.

_____ 1. A <u>chicken's</u> egg is an omelette's main ingredient.
  A singular
  B plural

_____ 2. The <u>sun's</u> rays heat the atmosphere of our planet.
  A singular
  B plural

_____ 3. We hunted for the <u>birds'</u> nests.
  A singular
  B plural

_____ 4. <u>Italy's</u> shape resembles a person's boot.
  A singular
  B plural

_____ 5. My brother went to the <u>men's</u> locker room.
  A singular
  B plural

_____ 6. The <u>cities'</u> parks are for everyone.
  A singular
  B plural

_____ 7. The <u>trucks'</u> tires all needed air.
  A singular
  B plural

_____ 8. During August the <u>stores'</u> windows displayed back-to-school sale items.
  A singular
  B plural

_____ 9. The <u>oak's</u> acorns are the favorite food of a wild pig.
  A singular
  B plural

_____ 10. The strings of the harp are plucked by the <u>player's</u> fingertips.
  A singular
  B plural

_____ 11. The <u>cow's</u> grazing field was burned in a grass fire.
  A singular
  B plural

_____ 12. The <u>volcano's</u> eruption threatened the city.
  A singular
  B plural

_____ 13. The <u>teachers'</u> lounge has a coffee pot and microwave.
  A singular
  B plural

_____ 14. The <u>taxi's</u> meter determines the fare the passenger has to pay.
  A singular
  B plural

_____ 15. The dead <u>snail's</u> shell becomes a house for a crab.
  A singular
  B plural

Name _____ Date _____

# CHAPTER 31  Apostrophes

**EXERCISE** Decide if the underlined word in each sentence of the following paragraph is singular or plural. Write S if the word is singular or P if it is plural on the lines below.

(1) <u>Animals'</u> traits can be interesting. (2) A <u>spider's</u> web is actually stronger than steel. (3) Young kangaroos sleep in their <u>mothers'</u> pouches. (4) A <u>beaver's</u> teeth never stop growing. (5) <u>Monkeys'</u> tails wrap around branches. (6) The <u>geese's</u> feathers will fill a pillow. (7) A <u>lamb's</u> wool may become a boy's sweater. (8) A <u>squirrel's</u> nest is often located in the very top of a tree's crown. (9) <u>Wolves'</u> howls can be heard as far as ten miles away. (10) A <u>grasshopper's</u> appetite makes it a pest to farmers. (11) A <u>giraffe's</u> cud is somewhat like the cud of a cow. (12) <u>Giraffes'</u> necks are over six feet long. (13) A cuckoo lays its eggs in other <u>birds'</u> nests. (14) <u>Mice's</u> nests are lined with soft materials. (15) <u>Crickets'</u> wonderful chirping sounds are made only by the males. (16) <u>Alligators'</u> eggs are often hidden on the bank of a river.

1. _____
2. _____
3. _____
4. _____
5. _____
6. _____
7. _____
8. _____
9. _____
10. _____
11. _____
12. _____
13. _____
14. _____
15. _____
16. _____

Name _____ Date _____

## CHAPTER 31  Possessive Forms of Pronouns

**[31A.4]** Do not add an apostrophe to form the possessive of a personal pronoun.
**[31A.5]** Add 's to form the possessive of an indefinite pronoun.

> **EXERCISE** Write C if the correct possessive form is used in the sentence. Write I if an incorrect form is used.

_____ 1. Is anyones experiment complete yet?

_____ 2. Chandler didn't start his's until Thursday night.

_____ 3. Jesse and Jennifer are already finished with theirs.

_____ 4. No ones project won at the science fair.

_____ 5. Does your house have air-conditioning?

_____ 6. The dog could walk, but its leg was swollen.

_____ 7. Melanie and I baked our's together.

_____ 8. Is your's strawberry or chocolate?

_____ 9. Our new puppy is already housebroken.

_____ 10. Mrs. Murphy takes her's job very seriously.

_____ 11. We learned the lost kitten was their's.

_____ 12. Is this your's backpack under the desk?

_____ 13. That movie is everyones favorite.

_____ 14. I like this shirt, but its price tag is missing.

_____ 15. The house with the purple shutters was theirs.

# CHAPTER 31  Contraction or Possessive Pronoun?

**[30A.6]** Use an apostrophe in a contraction to show where one or more letters have been omitted.

**EXERCISE** Choose the word that correctly completes each sentence.

_____ 1. _____ no air on the moon.
   A  There's
   B  Theirs

_____ 2. Many grasshoppers sing by rubbing _____ legs together.
   A  they're
   B  their

_____ 3. An ostrich doesn't really bury _____ head in the sand.
   A  it's
   B  its

_____ 4. _____ late again for rehearsal.
   A  Your
   B  You're

_____ 5. A snake sheds _____ skin more than once.
   A  it's
   B  its

_____ 6. _____ quite bright during nights of the full moon.
   A  It's
   B  Its

_____ 7. _____ picture is on a five-dollar bill?
   A  Who's
   B  Whose

_____ 8. _____ moths, not butterflies, on those plants.
   A  They're
   B  Their

_____ 9. Ermines change _____ fur to white in winter.
   A  they're
   B  their

_____ 10. Many Scots wear _____ kilts on special occasions.
   A  they're
   B  their

_____ 11. _____ a bat in our chimney.
   A  There's
   B  Theirs

_____ 12. Are these _____ flippers on the dock?
   A  your
   B  you're

_____ 13. _____ the coach of the Rams?
   A  Who's
   B  Whose

_____ 14. The camel put _____ nose under the tent.
   A  its
   B  it's

_____ 15. _____ no milk left in this bottle.
   A  There's
   B  Theirs

_____ 16. _____ a halo around the moon tonight.
   A  Theirs
   B  There's

_____ 17. _____ a snake!
   A  There's
   B  Theirs

_____ 18. Did _____ team place second or third in the play-offs?
   A  you're
   B  your

Name _____ Date _____

# CHAPTER 31 — Apostrophes with Certain Plurals

**[31A.7]** Add 's to form the plural of lowercase letters, some capital letters, and some words used as words that people might otherwise misread.

> **EXERCISE** Write the correct plural form of the underlined words, letters, or symbols on the lines provided. If the form is correct, write C.

_____ 1. I can't tell your <u>a</u>s from your <u>o</u>s.

_____ 2. Toni wrote seven <u>T</u>s on her answer sheet.

_____ 3. Kyle's world is filled with <u>how</u>'s and <u>why</u>'s.

_____ 4. How many <u>s</u>'s are in the word Mississippi.

_____ 5. Tina likes to use a lot of <u>*</u>s in her writing.

_____ 6. Chuck's <u>4</u>'s and <u>7</u>'s look a lot alike.

_____ 7. People wore funny clothes in the <u>1970</u>'s.

_____ 8. You shouldn't use so many <u>and</u>s in your sentences.

_____ 9. Cullen makes his <u>x</u>s very small.

_____ 10. A chorus of <u>hi</u>s greeted the teacher.

_____ 11. Several of the <u>&</u>s were out of place.

_____ 12. All of the students with <u>5</u>s should join that group.

_____ 13. Don't use so many <u>the</u>s to start your sentences.

_____ 14. Mrs. Tomkins gave me three <u>I</u>s for incomplete work last term.

_____ 15. How do you make your <u>2</u>s?

# CHAPTER 31  Semicolons and Colons

**[31B]** A **semicolon** (;) is used to separate independent clauses of a compound sentence and to avoid confusion in certain sentences.

**[31B.1]** Use a semicolon between the clauses of a compound sentence that are not joined by a coordinating conjunction.

**[31B.2]** Use a semicolon instead of a comma between the clauses of a compound sentence if there are already commas within one of the clauses.

**[31B.3]** Use a semicolon instead of a comma between the items in a series if the items contain commas.

**[31C]** A **colon** (:) is used most often before lists of items. A colon is also used between hours and minutes and Biblical chapter and verse, and the salutation in some letters.

**[31C.1]** Use a colon before most lists of items, especially when the list comes after an expression like *the following*.

> **EXERCISE** Decide whether each sentence needs a semicolon, a colon, or a comma. If the sentence is punctuated correctly, choose D.

_____ 1. Ransom Olds invented the assembly line Henry Ford just developed the idea.
  A semicolon
  B colon
  C comma
  D No error

_____ 2. Three good friends of mine are Mary, Bob, and Tad.
  A semicolon
  B colon
  C comma
  D No error

_____ 3. Did the sun rise at 615 this morning?
  A semicolon
  B colon
  C comma
  D No error

_____ 4. The town committee will discuss the following problems traffic, potholes, and snow removal.
  A semicolon
  B colon
  C comma
  D No error

_____ 5. Elm trees produce flowers and maple and oak trees also flower.
  A semicolon
  B colon
  C comma
  D No error

_____ 6. The following animals have only one toe on each foot the horse and the zebra
  A semicolon
  B colon
  C comma
  D No error

_____ 7. In the drawer the detective found a gold pen, a ladies' glove, and a map.
  A semicolon
  B colon
  C comma
  D No error

_____ 8. Many wild plants produce pollen ragweed is one such plant.
  A semicolon
  B colon
  C comma
  D No error

# CHAPTER 31  Semicolons and Colons

**EXERCISE** If necessary, add a semicolon or colon to the following sentences. If the sentence is correct as is, write *no error* after the sentence.

1. The desk drawer held only three items a pen, a pencil, and an eraser.

2. Sea mammals include the following whales, porpoises, and seals.

3. Three popular breeds of dogs are setters, collies, and beagles.

4. The sailors are going to Boston, New London, and Miami.

5. On our trip, we took the following routes I-26, I-40, and I-35.

6. There really is a national groundhog it lives in Pennsylvania.

7. Many popular cars are made in Japan, Germany, and Italy.

8. The curtain rises at 8 every evening there is never any deviation.

9. Wild pigs eat the following plants, insects, and other animals.

10. I get news from four sources radio, newspapers, TV, and the Internet.

# CHAPTER 31  Hyphens

**[31D]** A **hyphen** is used to divide a word and to separate certain numbers, fractions, and compound nouns.

**[31D.1]** Use a hyphen to divide a word at the end of a line.
**[31D.2]** Use a hyphen when writing out the numbers *twenty-one* through *ninety-nine*.
**[31D.3]** Use a hyphen when writing out a fraction used as an adjective.
**[31D.4]** Use a hyphen to separate the parts of some compound nouns.

> **EXERCISE** Write C if the underlined words in each sentence are correct or I if they are incorrect.

_____ 1. Thirty two students in my class are going on the trip.

_____ 2. Three fourths of the class have access to the Internet.

_____ 3. Is this an up to date dictionary?

_____ 4. I like to go cross-country skiing.

_____ 5. A two-thirds majority decided the class election.

_____ 6. When will the president elect be inaugurated?

_____ 7. Gabriella was living in a dream-world.

_____ 8. Because of all the extra work at the office, I think my mom will have to work over-time this week.

_____ 9. David's four-cylinder car is very economical.

_____ 10. My brother in law works for the police department.

_____ 11. The return trip took forty-five minutes.

_____ 12. Congress needs a two thirds majority vote to override a presidential veto.

_____ 13. My great grandparents came to America from Ireland.

_____ 14. Those money-hungry thieves finally got caught.

_____ 15. Griselda's mother bought her an apricot colored sweater.

# CHAPTER 31  Other Punctuation Review

**EXERCISE** Each sentence is missing one type of punctuation. Write the letter of the punctuation that correctly completes each sentence.

_____ 1. Some actors like to perform in plays others prefer working in movies or televison.
   A apostrophe
   B semicolon
   C colon
   D hyphen

_____ 2. In a play an actor can get an instant response from his or her audience movies and TV do not provide that kind of satisfaction.
   A apostrophe
   B semicolon
   C colon
   D hyphen

_____ 3. The theater's director and management discussed producing the following plays *Hedda Gabler*, *The Cherry Orchard*, and *A Man for All Seasons*.
   A apostrophe
   B semicolon
   C colon
   D hyphen

_____ 4. Josh was very happy to get a ninety three on this math test.
   A apostrophe
   B semicolon
   C colon
   D hyphen

_____ 5. Kim painted several childrens portraits for the exhibit.
   A apostrophe
   B semicolon
   C colon
   D hyphen

_____ 6. Plots can be developed over a long time in a TV series plays must be performed in a single evening.
   A apostrophe
   B semicolon
   C colon
   D hyphen

_____ 7. Her new daughter in law is a veterinarian.
   A apostrophe
   B semicolon
   C colon
   D hyphen

_____ 8. Many people have hay fever it affects one in five people.
   A apostrophe
   B semicolon
   C colon
   D hyphen

_____ 9. Someones phone bill is going to be very high this month.
   A apostrophe
   B semicolon
   C colon
   D hyphen

_____ 10. Mandy is the best cross country runner on her team.
   A apostrophe
   B semicolon
   C colon
   D hyphen

*continued*

# Chapter 31: Other Punctuation Review *continued*

_____ 11. The documentary focused on life in the following countries Thailand, Peru, and Kenya.

  A apostrophe
  B semicolon
  C colon
  D hyphen

_____ 12. Only sixty eight percent of the students completed the test.

  A apostrophe
  B semicolon
  C colon
  D hyphen

_____ 13. Womens running shoes are on sale this week.

  A apostrophe
  B semicolon
  C colon
  D hyphen

_____ 14. I had thirty two cents left in my pocket by the end of the day.

  A apostrophe
  B semicolon
  C colon
  D hyphen

Name _____ Date _____

# CHAPTER 32  Spelling Patterns

**[32A.1]** When spelling words with *ie* or *ei*, the *i* comes before the *e* except when the letters follow *c* or when they stand for the long *a* sound.

**[32A.2]** In all but four words that end with the *-seed* sound, the sound is spelled *-cede*.

**EXERCISE** Read each group of spellings. Write the letter of the correct spelling on the line provided.

_____ 1. **A** believe
      **B** beleive
      **C** beileve

_____ 2. **A** neice
      **B** neece
      **C** niece

_____ 3. **A** peece
      **B** piece
      **C** peice

_____ 4. **A** thief
      **B** theif
      **C** theef

_____ 5. **A** receed
      **B** recede
      **C** resede

_____ 6. **A** deiceve
      **B** decieve
      **C** deceive

_____ 7. **A** acceed
      **B** acsede
      **C** accede

_____ 8. **A** recieve
      **B** receive
      **C** receeve

_____ 9. **A** eight
      **B** eaght
      **C** eighit

_____ 10. **A** frieght
       **B** freight
       **C** freaght

_____ 11. **A** superseed
       **B** superceed
       **C** supercede

_____ 12. **A** weight
       **B** wieght
       **C** weighit

_____ 13. **A** niether
       **B** neithier
       **C** neither

_____ 14. **A** leisure
       **B** liesure
       **C** leisiure

_____ 15. **A** excede
       **B** exceed
       **C** exsede

_____ 16. **A** foreign
       **B** foriegn
       **C** forieign

_____ 17. **A** hieght
       **B** hieight
       **C** height

_____ 18. **A** thier
       **B** their
       **C** thieir

_____ 19. **A** wierd
       **B** wieird
       **C** weird

_____ 20. **A** conscience
       **B** consieince
       **C** conseince

Name _____ Date _____

## CHAPTER 32 Spelling Patterns

**EXERCISE** Circle the correctly spelled word in each group. Then use the word in a sentence.

1. anceint/ancient/ancieint
   _____

2. speceis/speicies/species
   _____

3. sliegh/slagh/sleigh
   _____

4. earliest/earleist/eariliest
   _____

5. conveniant/convenient/conveneint
   _____

6. cities/citeies/citeis
   _____

7. feild/feeld/field
   _____

8. breif/brieif/brief
   _____

9. reciept/receipt/receept
   _____

10. ceeling/ceiling/cieling
    _____

11. protien/proitein/protein
    _____

12. seize/sieze/seizie
    _____

13. sucede/sucsede/succeed
    _____

# CHAPTER 32   Plurals

**[32B.1]** To form the plural of most nouns, simply add s.
**[32B.2]** If a noun ends in s, ch, sh, x, or z, add es to form the plural.
**[32B.3]** Add s to form the plural of a noun ending in a vowel and y.
**[32B.4]** Change the y to an i and add es to a noun ending in a consonant and y.
**[32B.5]** Add s to form the plural of a noun ending with a vowel and o.
**[32B.6]** Add s to form the plural of musical terms ending in o.
**[32B.7]** Add s to form the plural of words that were borrowed from the Spanish language.
**[32B.8]** The plurals of nouns ending in a consonant and o do not follow a regular pattern.
**[32B.9]** To form the plural of some nouns ending in f or fe, just add s.
**[32B.10]** For some nouns ending in f or fe, change the f to v and add es.
**[32B.11]** The letter s or es is added to the end of most compound nouns to make them plural.
**[32B.12]** When the main word in a compound noun appears first, that word is made plural.
**[32B.13]** To form the plurals of many numerals, letters, symbols, and words used as words, add an s.
**[32B.14]** Irregular plurals are not formed by adding s or es.
**[32B.15]** Some nouns have the same form for singular and plural.

**EXERCISE** Write the letter of the correct spelling on the line provided.

_____ 1. **A** ladys
   **B** ladies
   **C** ladyies

_____ 2. **A** dishs
   **B** dishies
   **C** dishes

_____ 3. **A** foxes
   **B** foxis
   **C** foxies

_____ 4. **A** kissies
   **B** kisss
   **C** kisses

_____ 5. **A** mazes
   **B** mazies
   **C** mazis

_____ 6. **A** waltzes
   **B** waltzies
   **C** waltzis

_____ 7. **A** ashs
   **B** ashes
   **C** ashies

_____ 8. **A** croses
   **B** crosss
   **C** crosses

_____ 9. **A** canaries
   **B** canaryes
   **C** canarys

_____ 10. **A** reflexies
   **B** reflexes
   **C** reflexs

_____ 11. **A** anxietys
   **B** anxietyes
   **C** anxieties

_____ 12. **A** stitchs
   **B** stitchies
   **C** stitches

*continued*

## Chapter 32: Plurals continued

_____ 13. **A** trollies
      **B** trolleys
      **C** trollees

_____ 14. **A** discoveries
      **B** discoverys
      **C** discoveryes

_____ 15. **A** speechies
      **B** speechs
      **C** speeches

_____ 16. **A** radioes
      **B** radios
      **C** radiois

_____ 17. **A** kangarooes
      **B** kangaroos
      **C** kangaroes

_____ 18. **A** potatoos
      **B** potatos
      **C** potatoes

_____ 19. **A** tornados
      **B** tornadeos
      **C** tornadoos

_____ 20. **A** tacoes
      **B** tacos
      **C** tacois

## CHAPTER 32  Plurals

**EXERCISE**  Write the correct plural form of the noun in parantheses.

1. Three musicians played (solo) _____ at the concert.

2. She was very respectful of the (belief) _____ of others.

3. The two young (wife) _____ talked on the patio.

4. The police caught the (thief) _____ who'd been stealing bikes.

5. Goblins, fairies, giants, and (elf) _____ all played a part in the story.

6. Shelley cut the grapefruit into (half) _____.

7. The butter (knife) _____ fell out of the drawer.

8. My cousin Bill rides bucking broncos at (rodeo) _____.

9. The (goose) _____ flew over the marsh.

10. We saw three newborn (calf) _____ at Grandpa's dairy farm.

11. The (child) _____ enjoyed riding the merry-go-round.

12. The (mouse) _____ ate all the cheese.

13. (Leaf) _____ blew across the sidewalk.

14. Hail damaged the (roof) _____ of several houses.

15. I've seen both red and silver (fox) _____ in these woods.

Name _____  Date _____

## CHAPTER 32 — Prefixes and Suffixes

**[32C]** The spelling of a base word may change when you add a suffix.

**[32C.1]** Drop the final *e* before a suffix that begins with a vowel.

**[32C.2]** Keep the final *e* in words that end in *ce* or *ge* if the suffix begins with an *a* or *o*. The *e* keeps the sound of the *c* or *g* soft before these vowels.

**[32C.3]** Keep the final *e* when adding a suffix that begins with a consonant.

**[32C.4]** To add a suffix to most words ending in a vowel and *y*, keep the *y*.

**[32C.5]** To add a suffix to most words ending in a consonant and *y*, change the *y* to *i* before adding the suffix. However, do not drop the *y* when adding the suffix *–ing*.

**[32C.6]** Double the final consonant in a word before adding a suffix only when *all three* of the following are true:

(1) The suffix begins with a vowel.
(2) The base word has only one syllable *or* is stressed on the last syllable.
(3) The base word ends in one consonant preceded by a vowel.

**EXERCISE** Write the letter of the correct spelling on the line provided.

_____ 1.  A saveing
      B savieing
      C saving

_____ 2.  A nervous
      B nerveous
      C nervious

_____ 3.  A closest
      B closiest
      C clossest

_____ 4.  A statment
      B statiment
      C statement

_____ 5.  A creatd
      B creatied
      C created

_____ 6.  A pricless
      B priceless
      C pricieless

_____ 7.  A truly
      B truley
      C trulie

_____ 8.  A argument
      B arguement
      C arguiement

_____ 9.  A plaful
      B playful
      C playfull

_____ 10. A hurryed
      B hurried
      C huried

_____ 11. A relyable
      B relyiable
      C reliable

_____ 12. A ireggular
      B irregular
      C iregular

*continued*

## Chapter 32: Prefixes and Suffixes continued

_____ 13. A smileing
      B smilying
      C smiling

_____ 14. A driving
      B drivving
      C driveing

_____ 15. A merryly
      B merrily
      C merrylie

_____ 16. A careful
      B carful
      C carefull

_____ 17. A placment
      B placement
      C placiement

_____ 18. A hiting
      B hiteting
      C hitting

_____ 19. A beginning
      B begining
      C beggining

_____ 20. A slimist
      B slimest
      C slimmest

# CHAPTER 32  Prefixes and Suffixes

**EXERCISE** Circle the correctly spelled word in each sentence.

1. The (waitier/**waiter**/wayter) dropped a tray of glasses.

2. I keep (sliping/slipeing/**slipping**) on that little rug by the door.

3. It was a very (**forgettable**/forgetable/forggetable) movie.

4. The (dipier/**dipper**/diper) for the water is near the bucket.

5. Once he caught the pass, he was (unstopable/unstopiable/**unstoppable**).

6. Maria and Haruki are exceptionally (**graceful**/gracful/gracefull) dance partners.

7. The soldiers were very (couragous/couragious/**courageous**).

8. The suspect's (denyial/deniel/**denial**) sounded sincere.

9. Grandma is (**staying**/staing/stayying) with Aunt Helen.

10. Mom's new casserole (createon/createion/**creation**) was delicious.

11. Thanksgiving is a (**joyous**/joyus/joyious) holiday.

12. Al is (**dissatisfied**/disatisfied/disatissfied) with his math grades.

13. Everyone enjoyed the (sillyness/sillinness/**silliness**) of the costume party.

14. Neela wore a very (tastful/tastfull/**tasteful**) black dress to the event.

15. Both sides of the issue were clearly (**arguable**/argueable/argguable).

Name _____  Date _____

# CHAPTER 32  Spelling Review

**EXERCISE** Underline the misspelled word in each sentence. Write the correct spelling on the lines provided.

(1) Jay had been saveing for a new racing bike for a long time. (2) The kind he wanted was well known for its exceptionally light wieghit. (3) Jay trulie believed that a lighter bike would greatly help his speed. (4) When he finally got the bike, he was dissatissfied with the results at first. (5) What was really upsseting was that his times showed no improvement at all. (6) His cousin Eric, an experienced racer, told him not to feel so hurryed. (7) Eric said Jay and his new bike needed time "to get acquaintted," like new friends. (8) "Besides," Eric said, "if you decide the bike's not right for you, you still have your reciept." (9) For a time, Jay still prefered his old bike. (10) He felt he'd made a mistake in his pursuet of the perfect machine. (11) But as he practiced on both bikes, he found himself moving faster and faster on the new bike. (12) It was also less fatigueing to ride. (13) Jay soon decided his judgement had been pretty good after all. (14) His new bike was an excelent choice.

1. _____
2. _____
3. _____
4. _____
5. _____
6. _____
7. _____
8. _____
9. _____
10. _____
11. _____
12. _____
13. _____
14. _____

# APPENDIX  Power Rules

**[Rule 1]** Use only one negative form for a single negative idea.
**[Rule 10]** For sound-alikes and certain words that sound almost alike, choose the word with your intended meaning.

> **EXERCISE** Read the paragraph and study the words in parentheses. Choose the correct words and write them on the lines below.

(1) I hadn't (never, ever) been to camp before this summer. (2) I'd (heard, herd) that it could be lots of fun, but it was even better than anything I'd imagined. (3) One really hot afternoon, we put on our swimsuits and had a water balloon "battle" to cool off—there couldn't have been (anything, nothing) more fun than that. (4) All the camp counselors were really great (to, too, two). (5) (They're, there) all college kids who went to camp here in the past. (6) It seemed like there wasn't (nothing, anything) they didn't know about canoeing, building campfires, and organizing really great games. (7) (Its, it's) a sure thing that I want to go to camp again next year. (8) You should come too; (you're, your) sure to like it!

1. _____
2. _____
3. _____
4. _____
5. _____
6. _____
7. _____
8. _____

Name _____  Date _____

## APPENDIX  Power Rules

**[Rule 2]** Use mainstream past tense forms of regular and irregular verbs.
**[Rule 6]** Use a consistent verb tense except when a change is clearly necessary.

> **EXERCISE** Read the paragraph and study the words in parentheses. Choose the correct words and write them on the lines below.

(1) The annual grade 7 field trip to the Albertson History Museum (occurred, occur) on a Friday this year. (2) Students were (told, tell) to study the exhibit on life in the 1800s. (3) They were supposed to (take, have took) notes on the exhibit. (4) They (saw, seen) the clothes people wore then. (5) They (view, viewed) wood-burning stoves. (6) They even (sat, sitted) in carriages and wagons that were once drawn by horses. (7) The museum guide (allowed, allows) students to sit in one of the desks in the old one-room schoolhouse too. (8) Everyone laughed when one of the boys (tried, tries) sitting down in the model outhouse. (9) On the way out, some students (buy, bought) postcards in the gift shop to help remember what they had seen. (10) The following Monday students (wrote, write) reports on what they had learned.

1. _____
2. _____
3. _____
4. _____
5. _____
6. _____
7. _____
8. _____
9. _____
10. _____

# APPENDIX Power Rules

**[Rule 3]** Use verbs that agree with the subject.
**[Rule 4]** Use subject forms of pronouns in subject position. Use object forms of pronouns in object position.

**EXERCISE** Read the paragraph and study the words in parentheses. Choose the correct words and write them on the lines below.

(1) Every summer my family (goes, go) to visit my grandmother. (2) (Her, She) and our Great Aunt Thelma have a cabin at Gull Lake. (3) During the day (we, us) swim and waterski in the lake. (4) At night everybody sits around a campfire and (sing, sings) old-time songs. (5) I like "Row, Row, Row Your Boat" the best when (we, us) do it in rounds. (6) My brother Ed (like, likes) "On Top of Old Smokey" better. (7) However, truth be told, carrying a tune is not easy for (he, him.) (8) Ed's not exactly tone deaf, but nobody ever (wants, want) to sit beside him when we're singing. (9) Even Granny (put, puts) her fingers in her ears sometimes. (10) Every time she does that, Aunt Thelma (tells, tell) Granny that she is being impolite.

1. _____
2. _____
3. _____
4. _____
5. _____
6. _____
7. _____
8. _____
9. _____
10. _____

# APPENDIX  Power Rules

**[Rule 5]** Use standard ways to make nouns possessive.

**[Rule 9]** Use the contraction *'ve* (not *of*) when the correct word is *have*, or use the full word *have*. Use *supposed* instead of *suppose* and *used* instead of *use* when appropriate.

> **EXERCISE** Read the paragraph and study the words in parentheses. Choose the correct words and write them on the lines below.

(1) John (should've, should of) stayed in bed on Friday. (2) That way he (might of, might have) avoided all that trouble. (3) Instead he took his big (brother's, brothers') new bike to Ambrose Park. (4) (John's, Johns') idea was to try out the new bike before his brother got home from school, but things didn't work out so well. (5) As John tried riding "no hands" down the big hill in the park, he fell off, and (Tommy's, Tommys') new bike got a huge scratch when it slammed into a tree. (6) Then Tommy came home from school early with a sore throat when he was (suppose, supposed) to be at band practice. (7) Immediately Tommy noticed where his new bike (should have, should of) been standing by the back door. (8) John (use, used) to be able to get Tommy to just go along with things like this, but not this time. (9) It will cost all (John's, Johns') allowance for the next two months to get the bike fixed.

1. _____
2. _____
3. _____
4. _____
5. _____
6. _____
7. _____
8. _____
9. _____

# APPENDIX  Power Rules

**[Rule 7]** Use sentence fragments only the way professional writers do, after the sentence they refer to and usually to emphasize a point.

**[Rule 8]** Use the best conjunction and/or use punctuation for the meaning when connecting two sentences. Revise run-on sentences.

> **EXERCISE** The following paragraph contains sentence fragments and run-on sentences. Correct each error on the lines below. Be sure to use proper punctuation.

**(1)** The seventh grade play this year is a murder mystery it's a doozy. **(2)** It is set in the 1930s three people disappear in the first five minutes. **(3)** Murders happen off stage it is not gory at all. **(4)** For costumes students in the play. **(5)** Tuxedoes, evening gowns, tiaras. **(6)** I play a duke and wear a top hat. **(7)** Carry a cane too. **(8)** Mary Ellen McGrath plays the Queen of Transrodaria. **(9)** A very heavy crown. **(10)** Mary Ellen likes playing the queen, gets headaches, the heavy crown. **(11)** Our teacher says we all need to speak more loudly no one can hear our lines. **(12)** I'm not nervous yet. **(13)** Maybe the day of the performance.

1. Revise sentence 1.

2. Revise sentence 2.

3. Revise sentence 3.

4. Combine sentences 4 and 5.

5. Combine sentences 6 and 7.

6. Combine sentences 8 and 9.

7. Revise sentence 10.

8. Revise sentence 11.

9. Combine sentences 12 and 13.

# APPENDIX Power Rules Review

**EXERCISE** The following paragraph contains errors. For each underlined word or phrase, correct the error on the lines below.

(1) I should of paid more attention when Mrs. Henkel assigned our social studies term papers. (2) Now I can hardly remember nothing except that the paper is supposed to be about our state's symbols and is due on Friday. (3) I checked with Sam, and he and I knows the state bird and flower, but that's about it. (4) I've also heard the state song, which the glee club sing every time we have an assembly. (5) Its got at least 39 verses! (6) Maybe I can write out all 39 verses Mrs. Henkel will think I've put a lot of work into my paper. (7) Maybe she'll think there's more to it than they're really is. (8) I should have went to the library last week to find out more about our state's symbols. (9) Believe me, next time. Pay better attention.

1. _____
2. _____
3. _____
4. _____
5. _____
6. _____
7. _____
8. _____
9. _____

# NOTES

# NOTES